GAGAKU READER

THE LIFE AND POETRY OF
STEVE RICHMOND

EDITED BY
KURT NIMMO & TODD KALINSKI

BUSTED DHARMA BOOKS

Acknowledgements

The poetry in this collection was taken from the following chapbooks and magazines. Grateful acknowledgement to the editors and publishers:

Earth Rose
Earth Books, 1974

Red Work, Black Widow
Duck Down Press, 1976

Wild Seed
Second Coming Press, 1977

Stance Magazine
Edited by Steve Richmond, 1980

Prospects
Wormwood #91, 1983

Gagaku
Planet Detroit, 1985

Gagaku Avenue
Limited Editions Press, 1986

Santa Monica Poems
Sun Dog Press, 1987

Demon Notebook
Water Row Press, 1988

A Simple Cretin's Therapy
Guts #2, 1989

Poetry by Steve Richmond
Guts #5, 1989

5.0L Poems
Sun Dog Press, 1991

My Wife
Deadtree Press, 1993

Steve Richmond Special
Riot of the Ants #1, 1994

The Poets Are All Liars
Stovepiper #1, 1994

I Am Full of Murder
BGS Press, 1995

Table of Contents

Preface
Kurt Nimmo

I did not have the chance to meet Steve Richmond. He lived in Santa Monica, California, and I lived in Detroit, Michigan. In a letter Charles Bukowski told me Detroit was nowhere, something like the asshole of the earth. I lived there and ran a literary magazine, *Planet Detroit*, a jewel in the asshole of the earth.

It was in the mid-1980s. I lived in a walk-up flat in a crumbling old two-story house on the westside of what was then the Murder Capital. The flat was given over to books, magazines and art equipment with a space carved out for my cheap Japanese electric typewriter.

I don't recall the first submission sent by Steve. I'm not sure if it was before or after the Bukowski chapbook I published. Richmond submitted a lot of poetry. He sent out large manuscripts. Poetry was his life—along with drugs, heroin mostly. In letters he explained how he put Gagaku music on the record player and sat down before the typewriter and wrote one poem after another. Gagaku is ancient imperial Japanese court music. It inspired him to write tens of thousands of poems. Steve talks about it in an interview with Ben Pleasants, included in this book.

I worked as a press operator in a printing factory, so all the paper and ink I needed for the magazine and the chapbooks was available. The company had no idea it was contributing to American literary tradition.

I decided to publish a Richmond chapbook. Steve sent a big fat manuscript. I went through the manuscript and picked out a couple dozen of the best.

Gagaku appeared in 1985 under the *Planet Detroit Chapbooks* imprint. The thin collection has a light lavender card stock cover printed with rhododendron red ink and an illustration by Allen Berlinski. On the back cover there is a photo of Richmond in a pair of sunglasses and a quotation by Bukowski: "I am sympathetic with Richmond's poetry because here, a good 20 years older, I feel much the same way."

I sent a batch to Steve and most of the remainder went to magazine subscribers. 30 years later, I have three or four copies.

In 1987 I decided to do another number by Richmond. He was excited about the project. But then a series of things happened, including a run-in with the cops that cost me a lot of money, problems with my job and also a break-up with a girlfriend. Suddenly I no longer had interest in the chapbook or much of anything else. I wrote Steve and told him I wouldn't be publishing the chapbook. I tried to explain, but knew he would be pissed and take it as a betrayal.

He didn't write back. Instead he found my phone number and called me. I was at work when he called. Richmond left a message on my answering machine.

He angrily told me to send back every letter, manuscript and book he'd ever sent me. I didn't respond to his request and I never heard from Steve Richmond again.

Fast forward twenty-five years. I was married, living in New Mexico and no longer involved with the poetry scene or publishing small literary magazines. I received an email from a friend informing me that Steve had passed away.

Some time later I happened across a Ben Pleasants' interview on the internet, *Twilight of a Dope Fiend*, and also Mike Daily's piece *Gagaku Meat: The Steve Richmond Story*.

Daily writes that Richmond had lost everything and was basically homeless. He'd blown through a family inheritance of a couple million dollars—mostly on women, drugs, cars, furniture and other lavish expenses. By the late 2000s he was living in a residency motel in East Santa Monica, a seedy place inhabited by crack addicts and what Pleasants describes as a few "Thelonious Monk like souls."

Richmond wrote his last odes here. He was forced to leave after the motel was raided by police in 2007.

"That's when Steve hooked up with the community charity service at St. Joseph's," a photographer friend, David Garcia, told Mike Daily. "They took him in and fed him and gave him a place to stay, and then from that he went to this rehab for six months in Santa Monica—150 men in one big room. By following through on that program, Steve had psychological counseling. And then he got the apartment in Venice. The city set him up in this apartment where he is living now, a couple blocks from the ocean."

Two years later Steve was dead. After learning of this I decided to make good on my broken promise and publish another book. Not a chapbook this time, but a trade paperback.

This book may be of interest to fans of the late Charles Bukowski, who is the most read poet in America right now. I decided to edit and publish this book not as a sideshow to the Bukowski phenomena, but rather because Steve deserves a final tribute and, also, without it much of his poetry—exclusively published by obscure small presses and magazines—would be ultimately lost.

This book would not have been impossible without the help of several people. Cheryl Townsend, the former editor of *Implosion Press*, provided a number of rare chapbooks and the photograph of Richmond on the front cover; Allen Berlinski, the publisher of *Sun Dog Press*, sent books and an unpublished manuscript and also gave advice; Todd Kalinski, the publisher of *Deadtree Press*, sent along a copy of Richmond's *My Wife*, selections of which appear here; Mike Daily, who wrote a definitive piece on Richmond, *Gagaku Meat: The Steve Richmond Story*, sent *Stovepiper*, an anthology of poetry and fiction that includes a large selection of Richmond poems, several which appear in this book; Mark Hartenbach sent selections from an unpublished Richmond manuscript; Doug Mumm, an old fellow small press collaborator, provided a copy of *Wild Seed*; and others offered encouragement and financial support, including Ron Androla, Andy Rasmusson, Haze McElhenny, Patricia Saunders, Jan Normandale, Rick Lupert and others, many from Androla's *Pressure Press Presents* poetry group on Facebook.

3

Twilight of a Dope Fiend
Ben Pleasants

Out there is the poetry establishment. They decide. I could give you a fistful of names. Worms in a bottle, Bukowski called them. They live off grants. They write for the I'll Review Your Book, You Review My Book Review. Each one has a chair on a committee from some mediocre American university.

For Steve Richmond, they were the poetry mafia, the grinning face of evil. They were clichés.

They didn't want a rich, Jew boy, rent collector on the inside rail. Steve did begin to cry. I can say that. I was there. It was sad. He was so alone on the westside of L.A., alone in his heroin poems and LSD demons. I drove him to the UCLA Medical Center for thorazine. It helped.

Richmond was an explorer of inner space. Like Thelonious Monk.

Hey
Hey, I woke up today!
And there was the sun again
shooting in through the shades
and spearing me in the eye!
And the clock! Still alive!
and the rug was not on fire!
and the lawn!
The trees! The gutter!
All there! Once again!
Today!

Press missed all this? Wow. That's all I can say.
Let's get down to method. Gagaku. Listen:

4

Gagaku

who will follow me here
no one?
no one comes here.
no one follows me here
no one hears these cadences.
I am quite happily alone
I don't even have
to smile.

The word that jumps out at you is cadences. Richmond's Gagaku poems derived from Japanese Court Music. He'd put on these rare Japanese court recordings. He got them from Kathy King at the UCLA Ethnomusicology Library. Bought them from collectors. Borrowed them. Brought them to his little house by the sea.

All his money draining away on rare books and recordings and punching bags and drums and colored chalk for his lovely charcoal nudes. And for his expensive and exotic and illegal chemicals.

The Santa Monica cops were always watching Richmond. They busted him over and over again. They busted him for profanity when he published his antiwar magazine with huge headlines: FUCK HATE.

"Smut Peddler Jailed" was the headline in the Santa Monica daily.

But mostly Steve Richmond was busted for drugs. His family gave up on him. Everyone did.

No one listened but Bukowski. They wrote to each other like lovers. Like father and son. There are more than 150 letters between Richmond and Bukowski, mostly written in the mid 1960s. You'll never read them. They've been censored out of existence by Bukowski Inc. The Richmond/Bukowski letters are bad for business. Bad for the Bukowski business. Bad for the rare book trade.

Ask the boys and girls who make the noise what really happened to Richmond/Bukowski correspondence. Say the rare book & manuscript market in L.A. Maybe David Zeidberg of the Huntington knows. Or Victoria Steele at UCLA. They once worked together, decades ago. Ask why they never speak to each other. Why they dance around the rare book market leaving Richmond's erotic demons on the shelf. It's possible they don't even know. The king and queen of the rare book market in L.A.

My most recent tapes were recorded after the mid-May, Dan Fante party at my house. A hundred people showed up for a reading of *Don Giovanni*, Dan Fante's great play about his old man and siblings and a possible ex-wife. I wrote the intro.

One guest, David Garcia, said Steve was fading fast. He arranged a meeting. I hadn't seen Steve in twenty years. We travel in different circles. I showed up at his motel room in East Santa Monica where he lives with a few Thelonious Monk like souls. This is how it went (edited version):

Ben Pleasants: Let's start with your family.

Steve Richmond: My mother and father died. My brother and sister... I haven't seen them for three or four years. They don't want to have anything to do with me. I was using heroin. For thirty years. I stopped using about a year ago.

Ben: I always thought you were the American Rimbaud. The most important lyric poet writing in America since WWII. Especially the Gagaku poems. They're the most important things you've ever written. Microscopic examinations of the self. They had a lot to do with the drugs you were taking at the time. The drugs were the microscope, I think. They allowed you to look deep inside.

Steve: I read that 99% of all art is created when the artist is intoxicated. I was exorcising my evil. It was therapy. LSD therapy.

I wrote thousands of Gagaku. It became an ego trip, going deeper and deeper into myself.

I said to Bukowski "it's selfish." He said "So, be selfish. That's what art is. Be a man. Be selfish. Go deeper and deeper down into yourself."

Ben: Bukowski loved those Gagaku poems. You went so far down into yourself with heroin and LSD, it was like looking into another universe. You paid the price for it.

Steve: Yeah. I did my work. Now I'm retired.

the demons teeth
are inverted and pointed
like lime circles hardened but white
and are glistened
the eyes are black holes
encircled by matter torn like a rag
only their tongues are red
lower lips are turned to orange
green spattered on lower fringes
staining upward like spider web
hoods of white cloth pointed
and flap with cotton muff at tip
in groups they clap single fingered gloves
gloves white but turn to leather
the seam turns red, blue is soaked all over
fingers scraping blue turned multicolor from the barrier
their teeth puncture the glass barrier
the glass cracks.

Ben: But the poems are out there. Al Berlinski printed a solid number in *Hitler Painted Roses*. You've published about fifteen books.

Steve: I know. I go online about once every five years. Get all the ego boost I need. *Santa Monica Poems*. Al distributed that one.

Ben: You gave me your first book, *Poems*, when we were at UCLA. 1964. You lived in Hollywood?

Steve: 1624 North Gardner Street. I went to Hollywood High. Played on the basketball team.

Ben: How old were you when your first book came out? *Poems*.

Steve: Twenty-two. I had a marriage that broke up after three weeks. The girl, Ruby, could never come at all. Hours would go by. I was a kid. I didn't know what was happening. I was all fucked up emotionally about that. Then Ruby took me to a reading at UCLA's Janss's Steps. There were 400 people. 308 were women. About 200 were foxes. I couldn't believe it. The guy's a poet. All the girls are attracted to a poet. I'm gonna be a poet. That's when I wrote *Poems*.

Ben: You sent it to Bukowski and he wrote you right back.

Steve: Yeah. He kept writing me. When I met him, he was forty-four, but he looked like he was eighty. He looked like he was gonna die.

Ben: You next book was *Hitler Painted Roses*. Bukowski encouraged you to write it. Was he your mentor?

Steve: I don't like the word. He was a Leo and I'm an Aquarius. He encouraged me, that's right.

Ben: He did write the introduction to *Hitler Painted Roses*. Bukowski loved the title. He loved Hitler. As far as I know, Hitler never painted roses.

Steve: He painted duplexes. He also painted paintings. He was a painter gone crazy. That was my point. A whole fucking civilization based on a lunatic.

Ben: *Earth Rose* was your third book.

Steve: 1974. It was my answer to *Black Sparrow*. They wouldn't publish me, so I published it myself.

Ben: In the forward, Bukowski wrote the following about you and your work:

"I like writers who are as strong as their work. That is the final test. I don't believe you can separate the man and his work. I don't believe that if the work is strong and the man is weak, that is all that matters. The strong man with the strong work will endure. No publishers have come to Richmond. The publishers are wrong. The work will endure. The poems you read here will endure."

Steve: I wrote a line "let the fags have San Francisco." I think that finished it for me with City Lights [Press]. I grew up in Hollywood. Where gays tried to blow me in the street. You know what I wrote about Neeli in *Spinning Off Bukowski*? He was down on his knees with his tongue out. Berlinski took it out of the book. Maybe I am a homophobe? Maybe I'm a latent faggot. I don't know. All I know is that I'm impotent now, and it's nice in a way.

Ben: Tell me about the *Santa Monica Poems*.

Steve: I was hung up on Kathy King. Katherine King. She came into the Candle Shop once and the sun was shining on her silhouette. She's responsible for the C.S. Lewis movies. Narnia. Her name was mentioned at the Academy Awards. She's an Aphrodite figure. She was working at the Gagaku Department at UCLA. Ethnomusicology. I spent one night with her.

Ben: Maybe she knew Jim Morrison?

Steve: She thought Morrison was a pig. I asked her about Morrison. He visited me about six or seven times during the years. He wanted to talk about his poems. The wizard shit. He was a serious poet. Just before he died he came over. A sycophant was driving him around. He was drinking Jack Daniels. I could see he was on the way out. Like me.

Ben: So you wrote a lot about Kathy King. She became your muse.

Steve: She didn't like it either. I lay drunk on her doorstep. I called her a hundred times a minute. She lived on Stoner. A little dive on Stoner.

Ben: When was that?

Steve: About 1975. She was the girlfriend of Sheldon Pearl. She worked at Open City. How nice it is to be out of all that shit.

Ben: I love your work. I just thought you were going to end up in serious trouble.

Steve: I did. Thirty years on heroin. Tracks here. I almost died. I have a hump on my shoulder. [A benign tumor as large as a grapefruit.] We're lucky to be walking around. I was in Brockman Memorial Hospital for five or six days. In the Psych Ward to get off the heroin. It helped. A friend got me in there. He told me to tell them I was going to kill myself. I pretty much was. They got me clean. We're both happy men because we wrote. I stopped. I could write another ten thousand Gagaku but who needs it? I'm tired. I was ready to die a few years ago. Met this girl. She comes and visits me once in a while.

Ben: You always like women. Bukowski had a love hate relationship with women.

Steve: There was a biography of Bukowski by a guy from England. Linda Bukowski didn't want me to talk to him. Sounes. She wanted me exclusively for her movie. I tried to get a thousand dollars from her not to talk with the guy. I was a drug addict. A power hungry Leo. Anarchist.

I left it there. I didn't have the heart to talk about the million dollar house he lost in Santa Monica. The house on the hill where he lived with his girl and his drug dealers. I wanted to remember the poet. The greatest lyric poet in America since Hart Crane. The poet and his demons. He's still out there in Santa Monica.

Morning
those idle eyes
sit by the seaside
all the lepers of insight
extinguished.

That was the way I left him.

American Rimbaud:
An interview with Steve Richmond

Ben Pleasants

Steve Richmond, Meat Poet, with more than twenty books to his credit, was Charles Bukowski's best friend at the time of their greatest production. Letters back and forth between the two number almost two hundred. After forty years of heavy drug use, Steve has reemerged to claim his place as the writer of thousands of Gagaku poems, a form he invented, and America's most important lyric poet since Emily Dickinson. I sat down with Steve recently along with an L.A. English teacher who was gracious enough to let us share his table and umbrella in the hot sun of Marina Del Rey. This is the first of three long interviews about Steve Richmond's life and poetics.

Ben Pleasants: You used to have a place up in June Lake or something? Didn't your father have a place up in June Lake?

Steve Richmond: No, they used to take me up to…Convict Lake… it's in the Eastern Sierras, … close to Mammoth, you know.

BP: The Sierras are so beautiful. How would you compare mountain climbing to the adventures you had in the drug trade?

SR: Very similar…

BP: … you could fall to your death…

SR: …[laughing] Aw well you know, we were all, in the '60s, you know we all, everybody, most people…

BP: Yeah but there's a difference, you were honest about it. You were one of the only people…

SR: Why do something… if you can't be honest about something, it's worthless. It don't mean if you have millions… what's the use?

BP: You did have millions for a while…

SR: The whole criteria I found out, a couple of years ago, not to get a headache. If you are getting headaches, you know, and maybe, maybe is a one equation is the more money you have, the more headaches you get.

11

BP: You started your adult life very young, you told me about this woman who was like a dementive [sic] who gave blowjobs to all the guys in the neighborhood, or something?

SR: Well, there were a lot of those [laughing].

BP: Do you remember that?

SR: Most women are like that. But, you know, they keep it a secret.

BP: When did you start with drugs?

SR: I started drinking in high school. Alcohol. Alcohol was a ... the first night, the first night I had... remember those little cans of Country Club?

BP: Yeah.

SR: Malt liquor? First night I... a guy took me to a ... there were two girls living up in the hills in their rich parents' house, ... it was my first time. And the first thing that I did was I walked down to the door, she was standing in the doorway, talking on the telephone... and I put my hand right on her crotch, and I never did anything like that in my life. That was the inhibitions removed by the three cans of Country Club.

BP: They kind of go together actually. The ecstasy of drugs and alcohol and...

SR: ...maybe that's why the alcohol monopoly keeps the... without alcohol, I guess there is no economy.

BP: [laughing] When you first got into drugs, were you in college? Or...

SR: Yeah. Everybody got in before me, that I knew, you know.

BP: Was it your fraternity?

SR: No, no that was just strictly...I didn't get in 'til I was about 23. Smoked my first joint.

BP: What was your fraternity? What frat were you in?

SR: Phi Lambda Phi. Rafer Johnson [Olympic decathlon champion] was in it.

BP: No kidding. Do you remember any of those guys?

SR: Yeah, I remember, you know, I never see any of them for 40 years now. I got in, and I quit, and then I got tossed back in. They had great parties. And it was a, Jesus...

BP: Steve and I met at UCLA, and it was, you did your whole undergraduate at UCLA, right?

12

SR: And I went to law school at UCLA. Got a degree and I took my first hit of grass in my first year in law school so. That probably [laughing] changed my direction.

BP: You read the law sort of sideways, directionally.

SR: Well, law school it can be kind of, you know, it's like teaching English, it can be kind of dry [laughing]. Plus I didn't have a good legal... I mean I could tell, these guys had, you know, some aptitude.

BP: Did you get into it because your parents wanted you to do it?

SR: Yeah, my dad is a lawyer; I had a position of, you know...

BP: And here's a guy who didn't hate his father, he actually loved his father.

SR: Yeah, my father's great. Taught me how to trout-fish, he wrote poetry, too, all about God. My dad, he's a good man.

My mother was great. They were married for... you know...I had great parents. I mean, they were great Conservative-Republicans...But they were landlords, I could tell when I was about 2 or 3 years old, money didn't bring happiness, not that poverty did, but I'd hear him haggling with my grandmother about what she is going to do with the property...

[talking with the "other" diner (OD), complimenting one another]

SR: [talking about Ben] Met him at UCLA...I just started writing poetry and they were having a, he was running a poetry meeting in the student union, and uh, I showed up, you know, I had just started writing and it was an opportunity to read in the lounge, and uh, Jim Morrison was there, he just got up with his poetry, before he was even making music.

BP: True, he was there. Uh, the thing about Steve though, he had done a book, and I got a lot of books and they were just shit, I mean really, really bad, but I looked at this book and I thought, 'My god, I've never seen anything like this.' I mean his poetry was so original, this was the first of the poetry he ever did. It was like, putting it out there, you know, to test to see what people thought. He sent a copy to Bukowski, who already was one of the most important poets in the country, and he wrote back right away, that this is really amazing stuff. This is 1964...

SR: That was '64. Yeah, I got some poems accepted the first time I sent out—I sent them three places: *Kenyon Review*, you've heard of them...

Wormwood, you haven't heard of *Wormwood* probably…and *Partisan*. Two of them sent 'em back and one of them accepted eight poems… just… yeah, you know, here I am, in my first year in law school and for the first time in my life, you know [laughing], somebody, you know, somebody had related to my soul… I said, 'I got to do this for the rest of my life.' This made me feel so good, I wanted to do it for the rest of my life, and I did.

OD: Strictly poetry, huh?

SR: Yeah, I threw out prose here and there. I tried prose but, you know.

BP: Steve is a lyric poet, that's what he is. Just like the great Chinese poets who wrote short lyrical poems. And one of the things that influenced him, I'll let him talk about it, was this incredible Japanese court music, called Gagaku, and in my opinion anyway, his greatest poems are the Gagaku he writes, I would say that in a sense, when he listens to this music, he's… sort of intoxicated by what he sees in his mind. But I've never read anything like it. There is nothing in the English language like his poetry. It's a lot like Bukowski and nothing like it.

SR: I wouldn't want to be like anybody else, you know. If you can't be original, do something else. This girl I was seeing, excellent artist, took me to the UCLA music building, down below the studios, and there were these Japanese students/musicians, they were rehearsing this Gagaku, G-a-g-a-k-u, Shinto music, it's imperial court music, so when Japan changes its emperor, over TV… that's what they play, the Gagaku music. And it's available at Japanese record stores…

BP: And they were playing it at UCLA, for Christ's sake.

SR: Well, they play it all over now, if you go online, you see…

BP: No, I mean you actually saw them do it.

SR: I saw them play, I heard 'em play, you know, I mean, and just her [Anna Purcell] and I, and these two chairs. She took me down there and they're rehearsing, you know, they're playing.

BP: Ethnomusicology, the department of…

SR: The Department of Ethnomusicology, in the music building. And I started, you know, when you are really moved, you know, tears will come to your eyes. That's happened to me twice in my life. For art, Goya's glorious black paintings that I saw in Spain. Something so full of, you know, something there, that I found a connection with….if there is an essence, beyond words. So I got the music and I started writing to it. … I titled everything "Gagaku." And I exorcised, I exorcised my demons, you know, I'd just pretty much come down and…

BP: And he also, attached to that his incredible interest in illegal substances, which really…

SR: You seem to go back to that topic.

BP: No, because…

SR: Well, because I became a heroin addict for 40 years.

BP: But an explorer. That's the difference. Heroin addicts are a dime a dozen, they're all over the place. None of them…wrote Gagaku.

SR: But I got it right…First, I was smoking grass, took a lot of LSD, but… you know, writing is the core. And, or course, if you are high, plus it was a social device, I remember, this girl picked me up, you know, at Beverly Glen park, two girls took us up, to Topanga Sunraid Acres, you know, but as soon as she found out I hadn't taken LSD, she just…ice [laughing] as a matter-of-fact, I had to hitchhike back…so I thought, 'I've got to take that drug.' For five bucks I got a double dose. I didn't know it was a double dose, he [the dealer] said take the whole thing. Did you ever take LSD?

OD: No, too risky for my day.

SR: Yeah, I mean I haven't taken it for 30 to 40 years, too strong.

BP: Actually, Morrison was also a great fan of Steve's poetry. Morrison became a minor poet, but he was a great admirer of Steve, I mean he showed Steve a number of his works.

SR: Oh, I don't think he was a great fan of my poems.

BP: Yes he was. Why did he come back over and over again to see you?

SR: It was, you know, because it was, he was a poet. He'd still be alive if he had stuck to poetry.

BP: He was very interested in your work. Are you kidding? He knew you were blowing down walls that nobody had ever tried to get into.

SR: Well, if you can't be original in your art, why do your art? Who wants to do something, somebody has done before?

BP: That's true. If you are a painter, you might as well be painting walls then, you know, if you are not going to do anything original. If you are a poet, it's the same thing.

SR: You're a poet. I mean that's how we…

BP: I'm just a scribbler; I wouldn't use the word 'poet.' I wrote for the *L.A. Times* and, you know, all kinds of magazines. But I did get a chance to get out there, when nobody else was talking about this stuff and talk about it. I did and I'm very fortunate that I…

SR: You're in up to your neck [laughing].

BP: But when you remember back to those early days, Steve lived in Santa Monica almost all of his life, had this little house on Hollister, you know where that is.

SR: My grandmother had all the properties in Santa Monica.

BP: Steve actually was the rent collector. He'd have to go around, and Bukowski loved this, he loved to rag him about that…

SR: Yeah, I had the Jewish guilt, I was raised in Hollywood, and before I knew it I was screaming at poor little ol' drunks trying to live in their store front, and I was just, you know, hollering at them for their last dollar.

BP: But he lived in this really small, and beautiful little house, that he kept very very neat, by the way.

SR: It's been torn down and turned into a piece of crap.

BP: While he was there, he did his work, did his art, his poetry, and he also did a number of drawings, paintings, and so on and so forth. I thought in a way, it was kinda like one of the great Chinese poets, like Han Shan or Li. Po. Steve Richmond was somebody who was like one block from the ocean. And Venice became a world for you. I mean he did a lot of very unusual things like 'Steve's Candle Shop.'

SR: There was this 5000 square foot vacant building, everything was vacant in the '60s—down there, you know, all the windows were broken. And I read that the buildings were $150/a month. I started, oh I had it twice: the first time I called it 'The Earth Rose,' I wanted it to be a gallery/bookstore, but people only bought zigzag papers [both laughing]. It became a psychedelic store.

BP: Now that you know about [both laughing]. And wasn't there a woman who was doing bikinis or something?

SR: Well, that was the candle shop. I got out of there after a year, and then I got back in though, two years later, for the same price, I had a…I was on LSD one night at my little house, in my garage, I was making candles, I had a barrel of wax. Do you ever see people dip candles? I got this idea, maybe there was about 11 wicks hanging, and I had been dipping them in the wax, and they were about a half an inch thick, I got this idea, why don't I weave them together. And then dip them, and then weave them together, and make three legs out of the wax, just form the bottom of the candle, and then when I'm through, tie off the wheel up here so that the candle is here and here is the barrel of wax. Put a cover over the barrel, heated wax, and form the three legs, lower the rope, so that the bicycle wheel comes out and the candle stands. I mean it'll have to dry… let it dry over night, and snip the wicks off, and you got a freestanding woven together braided totally impractical [candle sculpture].

[all laughing]

OD: You mean these wicks are individually light-able [sic]?

SR: Yeah, you light them all. But the problem is, the wicks go all the way through the thing. Put out a lot of heat. Plus it just melts all over the place. And the flame is about this big, long, [laughing] totally lethal, you know. But the first person to see it, the one I made, was a big bull dyke named BJ, nice woman, "How much? How much?" And she wanted to buy it. And I say 'Nine bucks, how's that?' And the cost, I figured it out, was about 11 cents worth of materials, things used to be cheap in those days… And from there…people saw the things and wanted to buy 'em.

BP: They were beautiful, they were multicolored, they were just incredible. Nobody ever saw candles like that before. They were completely unique.

SR: But I couldn't write. I ended up having the same store, I had 'The Earth Rose' there, I put the candle shop in there… there was a movie *The Mephisto Waltz*, Jacqueline Bissett, and this guy, the director would come by and he had seen my candles in the shop and wanted them for his movie. But whatever I was putting in the candles, I couldn't write any poetry. I mean I was a 'poof' [all laughing].

BP: What was that great Greek film? Steve had a real going-out-of-business sale, like you never seen in your life.

SR: Wow, Kathy King came by and some guy.

BP: Zorba, the Greek.

SR: ...I was totally womanizing... all the women that came in the shop, that was half the reason...

BP: This was Venice, and the woman he was sharing the space with sold bikinis, so he had all these women coming in to get bikinis. So it was like the biggest pick-up place in the world. Right?

SR: Well, no, well for me it was... Fat candles, totally phallic, you know.

BP: Right, it was male and female—bikinis and candles.

SR: Bukowski visited the place. He'd stay and watch the girls come in and look at the candles and say, "God, it's like they are hypnotized." But I got this girl... Aphrodite figure, who happened to work in the Ethnomusicology department at UCLA.

BP: Kathy King.

SR: Kathy King, yeah. And she was, you know, I don't know, the first time I saw her, I was playing chess in back, and all of a sudden this woman here, about 21, she wanted to buy a painting I had, a charcoal drawing I had of Adam's torso from Michelangelo's 'Sistine Chapel'... and I said that's not for sale, and as she walked out the front door, about 50 feet away, the sun was shining right through the front door, the silhouette, the silhouette of her figure, was just...

OD: All of a sudden, your painting was up for sale, eh?

SR: No, I was thrown aside, I was 'God Damn' you know, Aphrodite, who steals the wits and the wisdom of men, that's what it was. I told the guy I was playing chess with, and he said, "She was studying you," while I was studying my next move, he was watching her, she was studying me. And I said to him, I remember this, 'She'll be back.' That's how confident I was in my young days [laughing] and I had teeth. And she came back a week later, and I chased her on the beach, anyway, to make a long story short, you ever made love to a woman, you know, you're moving you know, and then she puts her hands on your hips, and kind of beckons you to be still, and then she starts moving below you, and it's just, and she starts singing like Circe, and it's just, it's otherworldly. It's better than 'Margot Fontaine', the ballet. I mean it's just, totally you know, metaphysical.

BP: I've had similar experiences, and you never forget them. It's the ultimate communication.

SR: It's too strong for us. And of course, I tried to get back, and made a fool of myself, fell on her doorstep once, drunk, and she walked over me with some guy, and you know, I… so anyway, and she got out of the ocean with some other guy and I'm sitting in front of my candle shop and you know, I put a little sign out in front that says 'Free Candles' and the whole neighborhood, just came in and grabbed these things, took 'em away.

BP: You know the Zorba, the Greek scene where they all come in and clean out the house? But there was a great article in the L.A. Times in the magazine, I think it was *West Magazine*, that did a whole thing on 'Steve's Candle Shop'—the beauty and the color of the candles—so that's there forever.

SR: I never saw it.

BP: Every opportunity that has been offered, and you didn't show up.

SR: I wanted to be, you know, if I was going to make any fame, I wanted it to be as a poet. Not as a candle-maker…I was hiding out, I locked the front door, and I didn't show up [laughing].

BP: But with Steve there is this collision—of color, especially in his art, and in his paintings, and his poetry, and drugs. I'm coming back to the drug part because… it's a very dangerous thing to play around with, it's like teaching a 5-year-old to shoot a .45.

SR: Yeah, almost everyone I know is dead—overdosed, by the dozen.

BP: And yet, it really shattered barriers, like you've never seen before, I mean, you think of Rimbaud, the great French poet, with alcohol, with… they broke through barriers with the French language, Steve really did the same thing… So let's go back to your second book, no let's just go back to the Gagaku: How many would you say you have written over the past 40 years?

SR: Eight- or nine-thousand. You know, just put the music on…about two weeks ago, I wrote no poems for three months, and then six in the last 14 minutes. They're very short now.

BP: I've always thought that the Gagaku form is sort of sketching, in other words they are very short things, like a person who does a beautiful line sketch, like Matisse or somebody like that, you look at it and think 'Wow, I couldn't do that.' And that's my impression, of what your Gagaku's mean, 'cause they are short. They seem to come in a massive wave, sort of almost like having a stroke, they just come flying out with all this stuff, and you get it all down, almost the way...

SR: That's the way it used to be. Now it's survival. I use it as a sort of last resort. When things really get... months will go by... I got the music right next to me, it's like math, it works. It's just, you know, time to write... usually lasts about 25 minutes. I don't even submit 'em anymore, unless somebody asks.

BP: People do ask.

SR: Yeah... this guy from *Orange Tangerine*, in England, read the piece in *Beat Scene*...anyhoo, he sent me a great letter, said he's doing this anthology ...sent me certificates for postage, I sent him seven or eight.

BP: Where is he from?

SR: London.

BP: Ok, that's great. You know what, fuck the U.S. they never get it.

SR: They'll come along, you know, after England.

BP: They're always the last, you know.

SR: U.S. is just, you know, into the election.

BP: Well, take a look at the publishing industry of New York City, it's basically run by about five guys.

SR: ...Bukowski picked up on *Ask the Dust*. You know, he picked up the soul and rhythm of the man's voice and added...and from there on it's a... you know, I was with you and Bukowski at his place once, I took you over to visit him. I remember Bukowski saying, "Ah, don't mention the title, don't mention that book." I was half asleep, and you said... I know he didn't want me to read *Ask the Dust* at that moment, because he knew I'd pick up on the fact that Bukowski was born in the Year of the Monkey, and "Monkey hear, Monkey say," he picked up on [John] Fante and he took that, you know, it's like me listening to Gagaku music for the first time, Bukowski reading *Ask the Dust* for the first time...it gave him a voice. I mean a new voice. Since Fante became a screenwriter, Bukowski had this great basic voice…to work with.

BP: He reinvented poetry because he used the forms of prose that Fante gave him and he wrote them as poetry and that really changed the whole world.

SR: That's what I mean. Which is great, which is great, you know.

BP: Guys that do cement work have a Bukowski book in their backpack.

SR: That guy's got like 20 million books in print now.

BP: Everywhere, that's right, and that's because he stripped it down to clean language (not clean in the moral sense, but just as he always said "the line," he got that line down there, this "the hard line" and he got it partly from D.H. Lawrence, who he really admired a great deal, but was a little more fancy…)

SR: 'The Prussian Officer,' yeah. He loved the brutality of that story. He wrote that poem about never being glad he never had to meet D.H. Lawrence. He was a son-of-a-bitch, Bukowski.

BP: There was a great thing that Magid, my friend, did. He runs *The Persian Book Review*, and he translated this poem, it's called, "The Whore who Stole all my Poetry." It's the story about a woman who, you know, sleeps with Bukowski and then steals a stack of his poems [laughing].

SR: Who Magid or Bukowski?

BP: No, Magid [Roshangar] translated it.

SR: It's a Bukowski poem?

BP: Yeah. On the left side of the centerfold of this review is the English, and on the right side is the Farsi, in that beautiful script. So he's the one who's kind of interested in doing a Richmond issue.

SR: That'd be great.

BP: Well, let's talk about one more thing, that I think is more interesting to me, um, which I hinted about and it's really painful I think to talk about it but to go through the whole process—when you inherited all that money, at the time you had your little house, and then eventually they tore it down or whatever, and then your parents died, and you inherited this money and had this big house. We both have the same publisher Al Berlinski, so he showed me the photographs—you had a pool in the back, you had a limo... Did you have a limo?

SR: I had a limo, I woke up one morning, I had a million and a half in the bank, I woke up one morning (I was with Merisha), I said, 'Yeah, I want a limo,' I went out and four hours later I had bought this beautiful, eight-year-old Cadillac. Got it in Beverly Hills, they had a bunch of old limos, just gorgeous thing... got it for $30- some odd, $32,000. After a year or two the frame dragged and I sold it for $3000 [laughing]. It was fun. Beautiful.

BP: The house was where?

SR: I showed you the house.

BP: Well, tell me.

SR: Euclid and... Hill...it was an 18-room house, cost me $700 a month to keep the pool at 90 [degrees], my legs, each one of my legs weighed as much as I do now, 'cause I was full of poison, from all the toxic, you know, stuff—crack and heroin I was doing, 'cause that's all I did. I played a keyboard though, trying to make music.

BP: You did some Eric Satie.

SR: There was a record of Satie's solo piano, that is one of the nicest pieces of music I have ever heard in my life, I used to write to that. Beautiful, you know, I mean a, great minor key, very, I don't know if you ever heard that, I had to go to this little record store...

BP: I haven't heard that, but I was much more interested in the music you were playing yourself.

SR: Like any idiot, I made a disc and had a thousand copies made, and I haven't had a... lost them all, I don't know where they are. Berlinski has a copy.

BP: I'm sure he has more than one. Al always files things away.

SR: But that house was, you know, if I had to do it all over again, that's the one thing I wouldn't have done. But I wanted to see what it was like too, you know.

BP: And what part did Merisha play in all of this?

SR: She had the uh, upstairs was the master bedroom...

BP: Did you love her?

SR: Yeah, but one day after 20 years together she told me, she says, "I'm just with you for the money."

BP: Geez, after all that.

SR: She's an Aries, and Aries women…will finally put their foot in their mouth. And as soon as she said that… I asked myself, 'What am I doing with this fucking woman?' [laughing] 'Cause she was a hooker when I met her, you know, but a beautiful…and she was a great painter…

BP: Where did you meet her?

SR: First time I saw her, remember the Lafayette Café on the Venice boardwalk?

BP: Vaguely.

SR: On Westminster and the boardwalk, back in the '50s and '60s. She was working, I walked in there one night, I had the candle [shop]…went down there it was dark, nightfall, and there was nobody in there except the waitress and the owner, this old Greek guy, when I knew him…and she was the waitress. She was striking, just striking, I mean just the way she moved, animated, you know, she was a… seductive black widow… just gorgeous. She was a witch. [laughing] She read Lautreamont, before I ever heard of him. And she lived at the top of this old three-story apartment house, it was like The Addams Family house, …almost to Santa Monica canyon, on Ocean.

BP: I remember that. It was a beautiful house.

SR: Morning Glories all over and it was magic.

BP: And she was on to a lot of illegal chemicals.

SR: Yeah, she was…main-lining…took me a year to make love to her. Even though she'd offered herself to me for ten bucks at the beginning, but I just, you know, I was right next to her on her bed, and she had goose pimples, and I thought 'This girl doesn't want to make love?' She just wants to get high… and I wanted it to be more than that…

BP: Because you sacrificed a great deal for her.

SR: She taught me to oil paint. I always wanted to oil paint, she told me to get a tube of zinc white, and a red, blue, get some primary colors. And she put down a big blob of the zinc white on a paper palate and just a tiny speck of red, cadmium red or something, and the whole pile turned pink, this little tiny piece of red makes the whole thing light up, you know, and that just opened it up to me, right there. I said 'God Damn,'...

BP: That picture you did with the unicorn was just a beautiful... I think it's in Lory Robbin's [Lawrence "Lory" Robbin] photograph. I loved that painting. I don't know where it went, somebody took it obviously. It's the one with the waterfall.

SR: Yeah... Bukowski... the only thing he ever asked me for was that painting, but I was too fucking cheap and stupid to give it to him.

BP: Well, it's out there someplace. At least, there is a photograph of it because Lory got a very nice shot.

SR: Is he still alive?

BP: Oh Lory's fine, you know. He's gonna pass on the photograph to this woman in Montreal. I'm in touch with Lory, you can contact him anytime...

SR: No, I'd prefer to talk to you, here for lunch once every, whenever you feel like it.

BP: That's fine.

SR: I told ya, I think, I was walking down to the little Santa Monica library and they had 15 different Bukowski books, and every time I went in there they had three more books...and I just burst into laughter. My god, you know, all these things coming out, it's just...

BP: Well, I think what's incredible: a lot of poets, while they're alive they are great promoters and they are out there and everybody reads them, and then they kinda drop dead. Because he's been dead for 15 years, for christ's sake, and his books are still coming out!

SR: Well, I told you his wife said to me, his widow said to me, thanked me for what I was doing, it killed me. I don't know what she was doing. I think it had to do with the *Love Bukowski* play and opera and all that stuff.

BP: Yeah, they were actually going to do a sitcom on Bukowski at home, or something like that. You can you imagine [laughing].

SR: I think she murdered him [laughing]. And I always figured, if I was the judge in her case (he was very difficult to get along with, I'm sure), I would hold her 'not guilty,' 'justifiable homicide,' you know.

BP: You're the lawyer [laughing]. There was one thing he did, that I think was very bad: he wanted to leave all of his money to his daughter…

SR: Yeah, but his daughter married a black kid, and he didn't like blacks, you know…

BP: He was from India. That's right, but in the end he left her nothing. I think what happened partly is that originally it was 50-50, half of it was supposed to go to Marina, and half of it was supposed to go to Linda, and she slipped him a piece of paper and he signed it, and it said all of it went to her. Had it been 50-50, it would have been a real problem, 'cause both would have had to agree about anything.

SR: She met him at a reading; he was a holiday drunk genius, you know. And she was running a health-food restaurant. And she was a nice woman, I met her, you know.

BP: She was not a nice woman.

SR: Well, to me she was. Sort of quiet.

BP: She was a vampire.

SR: Of course she was, they're all vampires… The problem he had, he should have known, a woman who'd never heard of [Robinson] Jeffers, was not a woman to marry. She's after him for… he didn't care; he's a horny old drunk, you know.

BP: I think, actually, Linda King was great for him in a lot of ways. I think she really cared about him.

SR: She tried to kill him. But out in the open, she tried to run him down on the sidewalk.

BP: When was that?

SR: You've read that, haven't you? He writes about it all of the time.

BP: I never believed anything he wrote.

SR: Linda King was a crazy artist.

BP: She was a pretty good, really good sculptor.

SR: Yeah, she gave me a sculpture once; it was a torso of 'Venus,' excellent thing. I broke it finally after a years of moving around…plaster of Paris.

BP: I never really knew her. I met her once…and then she threw all of Bukowski's stuff out onto the street. At Carlton Way.

SR: She threw all his stuff out, she beat up his girl, the girl he was with that night, she took his typewriter and threw it out into the street and stomped on it.

BP: I picked it up and carried it back in.

SR: She… tried to run him down while he was walking on the sidewalk. And then he…called the cops…there was a party she had at her house, about 50 guys… and about three or four women, and she was just flirting. Poor Linda King, she was just trying to make him so jealous, she was so awkward.

Oh, I don't want to be sued for defamation. But that's the rumor. I would say the chances are about two out of three that Bukowski was murdered for his royalties and that he deserved it.

[both laughing]

BP: Yeah, he would have been a very difficult person to live with.

SR: It's a funny thing, the way he wrote. When he wrote about real people, he would lie, but his lies brought out the truth in a better way, you know?

BP: Well, you got it right when you wrote that thing, '300 Poems,' where you said he turned the knife, he liked to do that.

SR: Yeah, so did D.H. Lawrence. He got that from D.H. Lawrence.

BP: Let's go back to you. It's interesting how Bukowski died; I guess we could interview the nurse.

[both laughing]

SR: He's probably living in Bermuda.

BP: Yeah, that's right, they paid him off. But tell me what happened with your house…what did you buy it for?

SR: My grandmother left the house and all the property to the five grandchildren, and I was one of the five. I lived in the house on Hollister for 40 years. She let me move in there when I was 19, for $40 a m…

BP: No, I meant the big house.

SR: Oh, the big house, I lived there three years. And, you know, basically it was a business…

BP: How much money did you inherit (if you remember)?

SR: A couple million.

BP: A couple million bucks, and so you bought the house, where was it?

26

SR: Paid $803,000. Sold it three years later for $975,000.

BP: Ok, what was it like living there?

SR: It was, you know, I totally screwed up…the master bedroom was upstairs with a shower as big as my apartment now. But I'd lock myself in there with my Shar-pei puppy [laughing].

BP: What was his name?

SR: Sweetie, it was a she. I ended up having to take her up to the Topanga Hills and just let her go, because she'd bite anybody that tried to…I loved that dog. It's the last dog I'll ever have, I can tell you.

BP: Jeffers wrote the greatest poem I had ever seen about dogs, and I'll send it to you. I specially printed it on a card, as a memorial for my aunt. So you lived in this house…

SR: And I had my girl, you know, she lived in the second bedroom, the second big bedroom on the second floor. And there was a hole, a closet between the two bedrooms. There was a wall, you couldn't walk through it, but…I put a hole through the wall, and I'd pass her outfits, you know [laughing]. So we'd pass things back and forth, you know, and then she'd come over and knock on the door, it was kind of a…she was a mistress, you know?

BP: Did you buy a lot of clothes, the two of you?

SR: Ah, no, I bought a lot of…what did I buy? I bought a lot of furniture, we had paintings all over the place, we had a huge living room, the whole second story was about, god damn.

BP: And you said the drug dealers moved in.

SR: Yeah, a couple.

BP: Do you remember their names, like first names?

SR: A guy name Nick. Nick was a poet, he's a poet/crack dealer. And he's a good poet…he was born in England, he came here, he lived in one bedroom downstairs. He'd pay us rent, $650 a month for the room—pay it off in crack, you know. I ended up owing him $5000. He was arrested five times. And then Calvin was downstairs about 6-foot-5 [-inches], black guy, 250 [pounds], a killer from the war, he was in Vietnam, Southeast Asia, Special Forces. Very interesting guy…he was like a brother. The closest thing I ever had to a brother was a stone killer.

BP: Wow. But you liked him?

SR: Yeah, yeah, but he died, God, he died last year…I wanted to get the hell out of there 'cause another girlfriend of Merisha, another crack-head, she starts screaming, at four in the morning, every morning, you know, just crazy. Crack-heads are crazy, you can't get any peace. And I was just totally spending…I was dodging…I weighed about 350 or something, and my legs, one doctor said I had elephantiasis, it was just drug poison.

BP: Were you writing much?

SR: I wasn't writing. I was making that music, and I don't know how that is, I haven't heard it for a couple of years. And it's just instrumental, you know, I'd go get stoned and did crack, you know, it sounds like a New Wave music.

BP: Techno.

SR: I don't know though, it might be very beautiful. Berlinski liked it. I sent him a copy of the tape and he said, "God, it's beautiful."

BP: It must be out there some place.

SR: Well, I'm sure he's got it in his closet.

BP: So you lived there for three years.

SR: Yeah, for three years, and I said, 'I gotta get out of here.'

BP: What happened to all the money?

SR: Well, I had the money for 12 years, you know, 12-, 13-, 14 years you can live pretty well for a million and a half, two million dollars, if you spend it well, probably $100- to $200 grand a year, $150 grand a year, until it was gone.

BP: 'Cause you had all these expenses—these people who were living off you. Did you support Calvin?

SR: Yeah, he drove me around and he was my bodyguard…I'm just reading this novel by Elmore Leonard called *Freaky Deaky*.

BP: Yeah, he's a great writer.

SR: Yeah, I've read about it. I got into his books about five to six months ago, and I've already read about nine to 10 of his books.

BP: He came along and said I'm the next big thing.

SR: The word 'Bukowski' is in this novel actually, you know, yeah he's great. He's really great. Start off with *Maximum Bob*, which is surprising, it was great. You know how it is when you are old, you come on a novel by a guy who has written 20 books, and you haven't read any of them. I'd pick his books up through the years, but I couldn't get into the lingo. Then all of a sudden I just, you know, got into *Maximum Bob* first, and went right through it. The guy's great. Great writer, plus, you know, he's fabulously wealthy, I suppose.

BP: Yeah, I'm sure he is. A lot of his stuff has been made into movies.

SR: Yeah, every time I open a book, I say 'Wait, I saw this' [laughing].

BP: So eventually, you blew all your money, and you went across the country.

SR: Went up to Oregon basically. Northwest. I bought a Contessa, Beaver Contessa, three or four years old, it was like a big RV. Beautiful RV. That's when gas was still reasonable. And I lived up in Bend, Oregon for six months in an RV place…

BP: Was Calvin with you?

SR: Calvin was, you know, driving the thing, and I'd sit there and shoot six needles a day and then fall asleep and wake up and then shoot another one, and fall asleep.

BP: Did you get busted up there?

SR: I've never been busted for drugs, you know. Had some very close calls.

BP: Never in your life.

SR: No, I was careful, you know. I don't know if it can be done anymore 'cause they've really clamp down on, you know, crack and heroin everything, you know. But if you want to you can get away with it, if you're very careful [laughing] and you're lucky.

BP: And if you have a bodyguard. Cops don't want to mess with bodyguards. Especially one's who have been killing people.

SR: So then I came back. Oregon, one thing about Oregon is all the dead deer on the road, it's like [Jean Luc] Godard's *Weekend* …I just came back and traded the RV to the guy at that motel—Sid Warshaw, you met him.

BP: Yeah I did, nice guy.

SR: And he gave me three years for the RV, three years to have my own room. Turned out to be four months short, because he got busted, the whole place got busted, and they kicked me out, the cops. So I was there for two and a half years, just plodding around with the crack hookers and I started writing there. Writing Gagaku again, so I was writing letters to that woman up north.

BP: So you were really reduced to one room? One room.

SR: Oh, I loved it! One room, just a garret—no broiler, no stove…

BP: And this beautiful woman who was blowing you? What was her name?

SR: Uh, Susie.

BP: Describe her–inside, out.

SR: She moved like a swan. I just looked at her once (of course, I was on crack) and, you know, said to myself (…tongue-in-cheek), 'She's the most beautiful woman in the world.' She said she liked to be with me because I made her feel pretty.

BP: So she was a poet too, huh?

SR: She wrote poems too, yeah, she was half illiterate…but it was interesting…

BP: Did you write Gagaku about the two of you?

SR: Uh, yeah, I wrote a bunch of poems, called her Aphrodite. Every once in a while, a woman comes along. I figure she's the new Aphrodite.

BP: She was in and out of jail for drugs?

SR: Aw man, she'd get together with crack dealers, get mad at them, steal their car, and crash it. While we were at the motel, she crashed four different crack dealers', I mean, you know, and the cops, she was notorious with the police. She'd ride around on her skates, you know, she knew everybody in Venice, she worked Lincoln as a hooker, she was 32 and I was 67…so I knew I couldn't keep her.

BP: But when you finally cleaned yourself up, you had to get away from these people.

SR: Well, when the police closed down the motel, my sister put me in a motel room for a night or two…

SR: And then I spent six months at Santa Monica's City Shelter, that's where I got clean.

BP: It's not bad, was it?

SR: Well, you know, I got bad bug bites, but I learned, you know, and there was... 120 mentally ill... and me!

Interview transcribed by Lisa Zucker

1.

with this work
I continue my life

gagaku

it is
not hard to do
        not
    even a candle need be lit.
merely move 4 steps to sound
        machine and put needle
                on disk
                gagaku
        ancient shinto Japanese sounds
                catalyst of my memory
my myth
    huge shadows like Goya's God in clouds
            moving.

gagaku

ah so I am deemed from the rich
ah so I am called
        too fortunate for my
monthly gift
ah so I am given almost total
            free time to write
    paint or lie about
useless upon some
beach

ah so 1 have walked down avenues of
                show window and washing machine
ah I have desired the rolls royce
ah I have desired the mechanical
bed waving and circling 3 robot
            venuses in
my sperm arms

ah I have fought my battle
    each morning
ah four years I have won
moved to writing

ah I am fortunate
ah I am not the poet
        who gave it up to be
            a
stockbroker
ah I am me myself
scribe.

❂

i tore my nails into
my stomach ripping a hole
big enough to put my hand
into me with blind fingers
feeling between intestines
and liver for the flower of
me, until i found it pulling
it out, holding it in my bloody
right hand until my left hand
got hold of my soul, and i
took the two and smashed them
together until they became a
solid piece of total beauty
for me to throw with all
my strength into the
stars

4F & FLUNKED THE BAR

it seems
I'm a stupid ass,
the army doesn't want me,
they don't want me for their law courts, I have been dropped
from the hand of God and am falling
                                falling
                        and I kind of like
it that way. To join any army I'd of had to forget
the hair on my nuts and my big
                                blood filled cock
                which screams I AM ME MYSELF HUMAN
                and will not join the shit games
inside someone else's
                        clock. Neither will I be
                the speaker of dead language . . .
        Have you ever seen a legal typewriter?
No exclamation points. Dead! A thing for monkeys who have
talked themselves into the rotten banana
of compromise. They took
                the first step
        because they thought they
could splatter their snailshit truth easier
                        that way, well
                that first step killed 'em & now they
        sit behind huge raised mahogany platforms
        with red white & blue draped over their shoulders
murdering murdering murdering.

gagaku

each
poem becomes a trophy,
my blood

each poem
is all I have,
women have deserted me—
all of them,
I sense
they hate art.

my blood,
each
drop

gagaku

table full of literary
crap, you bore me
yet it is these words
my own words
written to oriental drums
and odd instruments whose names
          elude me
   covered with paintings of
          demons in color
                    serpents alive and scaled
drums of my
truth,
I can't afford
to lie here.

gagaku

I lean back
in this wicker chair
no arm rests
my fingers on keys

I lean back
feel my back against
straw
where it belongs
I lean back

tap tap tap these words
I am comfortable
I lean back
listen and
transcribe my

life.

CELINE

let's hear it
    for him
  up there with
      Artaud Rimbaud all of them
        up there stinking
      in genius
         never gets off that
    flat rock
     good for him
        never the weakness
  always the strong word
      no gentleman
    here thank God
    keeps me living
  his medicine his words
       his cure
    his books his
      serum his
    spirit put face
  up on paper, good
     for him I
  say a saving
      grace for myself
      were it not
    for him on
    the high flat rock
       I might've
  fallen down from this
     cliff I climbed
    long ago.

gagaku

she in her place
me in mine

books of wisdom
have told neither
of us to move

I did move
however
counting on myself

and she
wounded me yet
I came out
of the war

bleeding
poetry

gagaku

field of flowers
I constantly see you
your yellow red blue green
and purple heads
waving in sunlight swinging
in breeze and
          peaceful under this blue sweet
sky.

swing in spell
 there is no curse on you
save beauty
and it is my eyes
that give you beauty.

it seems everything they have made public
everything that attracts large lines
in front of some box
office
everything that is constantly splattered
in newsprint
everything that is raised above our heads
on giant cardboard
everything that trails from tiny planes
in letters and everything upon the fat sides
of blimp in neons
everything of fame everything
of public notice everything
of cinema everything of television radio
public communication
stinks
unholier than shit
unholier than hitler's piss
unholier than anti-matter

it seems.

fuck i can not
yet describe
the blackbird in
the green tree

VISITED

                    buk
comes over showing
          off his beard

there are two women
          with him
they are sisters

one of them
        a brunette somewhat
slipped

and a great sculptress
      the other
a real estate agent

there's no reason
          to tell this
story

I did not want
      either
he wanted both

neither of them
            were the fantasy
I could chase

Buk & I
drank an equal amount
      of imported beer

Buk is doing better
      these days

when I first saw him

he had no more
     than one month left
and that was

nine years ago

gagaku

the act
is tiring without
passion,
and the women
are afraid of passion,
of being
swallowed whole,
especially the young ones
who arouse me

❂

i peeked
through neighbor's window,
and saw him in the kitchen,
with his organ in the toaster,
screaming

gagaku

a bunch of raving fucking beasts
that's what these poets are
I know
I've met them
I've looked in the mirror

gagaku

when the mystery
of another human
is gone, all we have
left
is another asshole.
these are my eyes
that isolate me

immortality

all I see about me
   dead
   especially those in the arts
it was not supposed
       to be this way

     I am forced
to pick up the living
     a being here
one there
   in my postbox

   I have traveled
    all about this planet
       and corpses
   abound in the most
    beautiful
geographical places

    those few who live
are so weakened by the dead
   that I know not
   if they too are dead
     and my weakened being
has lost discrimination

    oh I may be dead
     too
well, Mozart is still living—
  this
    a certainty—
   right now
he is telling
  me so.

Hey everybody likes me

one of those times in my life
when everyone I know
is on my side

I'm with them
they're with me
friends pure friends
not an enemy in the world
have you heard that before?
just a phantom
skipping through alleys
dagger in right hand
coming for me

and I'm not even a paranoid
everybody likes me
all my living friends
just a phantom coming for me

1 dead enemy
he hates my Jewish guts
thinks my cock a demon
he may be right
Celine punctuated his concept

is it too complicated?
don't you know what I'm talking about?
everybody likes me

gagaku

not a human being
or any living thing
without something
to teach

those teach best
who've no idea
they're instructing

just watch it move
more in the quick gait
of that small black widow
than in all

plato.

gagaku

I write about
      14 minutes a week
            condensed typing time

all these
      fools
        hunched over
           their machines

      paying for swimming pools
            money thrown to horses
              beverly hills apartments

bel air castles
    blond leeches

I write just the few minutes
      not to support your
          stomach
          not to
          support
   anything.

         it is all right
         to play pool
        if you can truly relax

        and the poems continue
            to spurt
        it is
        my old faithful of creation
          my cock my love my art
        they don't allow this sort of

goings on

in china
they would arrest me
for non work

yet I am inside the demons
describing my exterior
what makes evil tick

they don't allow this sort
of art.

they're coming for me
black smocks & casket carried
balanced on wingtips
strange white feathered arms
flapping them on here

leave it to demons
I'm their cargo
eagle beaks on their skulls
opening & closing
darting tongue
in and out forked
into 3 points
one red one yellow one
black

here they come
my brethren
their shoes fall off
their pink puds drop too
and out from the slit in their cloth
right where cocks have fallen
protrude a twosome of human balls

       white wrinkled covered with
black hairs thick as heavy wire
a real nest there

leave it to these demons
they'll carry me away
from this wonderful monde
long red nails
3 fingered claws
much like a chicken

here they come
th'first takes my nose
the next my arms
here comes one for my crotch
he's got my balls
the one after my dong
a female that one
now my legs
gone
there go my intestines
leave it to the demons

I'm on my way
back into th'rainbow
I'm splitup in pieces
nothing new

gagaku

now I know why they
           and myself
   visit the man
the pain of that man is great
        more than our own
and to visit him is to extinguish
            our own meager misery
(and increase his?)

it even makes me feel I'm seeing demons
           clapping
   constantly clapping
now weeping
huge drops of water
        ½ the size of their head
                fall from their two
                    blue eyes

demons with blue eyes!
        brown eyes too!
                red eyes!
here I'm controlled enough to see demons
        jacking off
        cocks
    the whole size of their bodies
                    rising ½
            their body length above
    their head.
here I am mad.

gagaku

listen
since you like
            my poems of demons
      I will write this:
       one with upper half of body
                  showing holds his two arms above
            his head and claps his
      hands likewise above
                  his head
            and roots me on
demons like to be described
                  they like to be immortalized
they like to be
written in poetry
they feel they deserve this.

gagaku

poor at the end of
 every month

the demons laugh at my
lack of funds

their hands (black shadows)
full of green cash

their faces are red
    a hot red orange
we could cook eggs on—

like sulfur springs in the sierra we
could put our hand

flat against their face
and scar our palms

permanently.

gagaku

I keep taking her and
                    she moves off a month
                    6 months
          8 months
and then I'll take her again
          she keeps appearing
   at intervals
always getting me
          aroused

there are 2
          3
maybe four of her

blond
   red hair
a brunette

all my dreams
          spaced

of course I play with demons daily
          they never leave
they *do* have staying power.

gagaku

more wood for the fire
                there's enough on
                        now for one poem
                                perhaps 2
        before I must rise
                        put more wood
                                upon the fire
        to stay warm
        in body in
            spirit

the women I love
                all sleep with other men
the women I love
                tell me
        they love me and not
                        the men they sleep
                                with

the women I love
                are asked by the men
                        "Why don't you live with Steve?"
the women I love answer
            "Oh I don't know if he would appreciate
                            that."

the fire is going strong
        the women I love
        will all be back
                long enough for me to
                hold fondle kiss
                        become
                                them.

gagaku

                        I want to write some brutality
                    I want to get my dirty little murder out
of me
I want to strangle my muse
                        her slim white body
                                    that moves perfectly
                                causing rise in
            my levis
                behind copper zipper

    I want to cut her balls off
                        massage my clitoris I
                                    want to jack in jack
                                    off jack out I
                            want to slay
                                    here now

62

gagaku

the crazy call me
   crazy
the rich complain about their
    poverty
  I have nothing to do
          save write my poems
  all else is taking shits
      acting the animal and pissing
    on territory

listen

listen we sacrifice the fame
stick to poetry
    make a move into prose
and somehow we've lost
        that certain touch

that shoe in my face
    it's the novelist's fame
that short story writer
    is only a short
story writer

listen we stick to poetry
we didn't want all that
        false publicity
all that crap to build a
            legend

listen we had a few hobbies
    we had a t.v.
we had a record player
    we had
a dozen healthy plants

gagaku

blake took the angels
                    cherubs
                    fairies
                        described them
            gave us joy
        and continues to
thrill our souls

I'll take the
        demons
        describe them
put white clothes on them
                    tell you of their jagged
                        clean teeth

how quickly their teeth
                    stain
                someone has to do this
        I'll be the hero

undecorated.

gagaku

this seems
        the only center
after all
    I fucked your wife
and you were very understanding
    I could
not be that understanding

here
demons play their brass cymbals
            clap them together
        and walk at the same time
                in slow circles
                    & slow figure eight

they all wear black
        gowns
they walk on a gray asphalt playground
marked with fading
yellow lines

it is daylight
the sun reflects off their black
    cloth
    in a dull way

the children are about too
playing dodgeball & volleyball
        or rather sockball
            (the ball is white)
the demons see the children and move among
    & through them

the children do not see the demons

and laugh and giggle and cry and
        continue to play

gagaku

to be able to come here
 middle
of this dark morning

        and write gagaku

what have I done right
              that this
       is possible?

I have pushed the woman
       who begged
 me to stop writing
     poetry

out of my life

gagaku

I need clear cool air
to continue

I need meat

I need women
clear ice blue eyes
white golden hair
a doe's radiant brown eyes
once again
clear marble skin
I need women

to continue

gagaku

today the sky is blue and clear
I have murdered three humans
in my last three poems
today is successful already
now I can rest.

gagaku

ho
how full I am
of bullshit.

ho ho how
arrogant I am.

ho shit
how often I jack.

how wearily I continue.

I have only 1 thing
        these poems
and they are not often
    strong enough.

I don't like the gay

you can say
it's my latency
& I'm over reacting
but I don't like the gay
you can say I lack human empathy
but I don't like fags
raised in hollywood
these fuckers of each other
trying to con me
when I was seven
I don't like the gay

now they keep out of my way
faggot assholes
chickenshit creeps

I don't like
        the gay.

gagaku

come now the demons
the wonderful demons
with their white lace
bridal gowns
long flowing dresses
trailing 15
or 20 feet behind
their black stench

oozing stinking creatures
the foulest things of this world
publishers of black sparrows
bubbles of a purple dark brown iridescent
        diarrhea
city lights bobbling about
  new directions all their lies
rexroth that fart I saw him read
and had to... I had to walk out
2 minutes into it
  it was that bad

now I'm getting hot
I am a huge globe hot red radiating
    I'm not the sun
don't accuse me of that
I'm close to Satan
  just to keep an eye on him

keep your enemies closer than your friends
that's what the script told
vito corleone to say

it makes sense
  terrible sense.

gagaku

I conduct experiments
my findings are reported
in small poetry magazines
                places where
the Art survives
    the only places

my experiments
are visions that I've allowed my imagination
    to portray before my eye

I merely describe in typewritten letters
what these visions are

I try for lucidity
I try for the simplest clarity

at the moment
there are no visions available to me
I wait a few moments

nothing is coming.

gagaku

ladies hold your country
                    and gypsy
aprons to the right

you have carrot red hair
        white freckled faces
red red lips
blue eyes
            green eyes also
ladies you are beautiful
I want to take off your dress
    feel your white woman's flesh
            warm against me
    I want to fuck you
ladies
each one of you.

gagaku

she comes weaving by
red smoke
something about her movement
        makes me want to
pump myself into her
right up

from behind

gagaku

mine was the shotgun technique
hell
I didn't even know how to spell
shakespeare was a puzzle
whitman didn't arouse
all those lines of shit
now I know better
those were men giving their best
        yet missing
and there was emily dickinson
    wonderful poem of death
yet I can't remember a line
  it was as if
we all spoke different languages
        under the heading English
finally a few tattooed themselves
    upon my soul
blake
anwar
a few others
it became my path
to fill a vacuum I sensed

        words never seen together
vision never imagined by any human
demons with red paint on faces and
        otherwise dressed totally
    in black robing
it became my project
  to describe their claws
        with three bony orange grey leathery
            fingers
yet fingers that looked nothing like human fingers
nails that were not nails but

long pointed talons
 I was laughed at
    unbelieved
put down as unfocused & irreverent
  and yet a few of my fellow
        humans
seemed to see what I described
thanks to them
these words are
 written.

gagaku

this is a working day
I have written many poems
some of you will take them
copy them on your typewriters
send them to a printer and he will
recreate me with your blessing
    I thank you.

2 MEN

I've just been talking with my father
he believes I should preface
my work
with an apology to all those
who might be
offended at my use of
profanity.

over the years I've talked at length
with Bukowski and
he feels my poem which begins
    with the line
"out of my asshole comes thick diarrhea"
is one of my best poems.

I respect both men.

gagaku

all the art's in the little mags
that's what they said
Pound Fitzgerald Bukowski
        all the others
they all said it
all the art's in the little mags

there they are
a dozen little demons
with black cloaks
        and in their black claws
                many many
            little white magazines
                    all with blank paper
            or a gibberish of black
    seemingly printed letters

they are fucking laughing at me

this is where I exorcise them
put my fingers into their rotting eyes
pus covers my fingers
there's nothing there but rot
rot.

gagaku

listening to gagaku
ancient shinto Japanese music
played for the imperial court of japan
way back when
and even now

they haven't changed a thing
same instruments same
sound
catalyst for my poem

only thing I know how to do
this quarter to 4 a m
put on the music
see what I see

big red oscillating radiating red ball
made of rubber
or a light plastic
could be the sun

against a clear blue sky
the ball is suspended above green ground
the ball breathes in and out
radiates its red

some black shadow
probably a demon
punctures this red ball with the
sharpened end of its broom stick
yellow wooden pole

more of an orange yellow colored broom
holding the brush end he

or she sticks the wooden end like a
spear into my sun or ball

his blackness is a depth blackness
something that I could crawl through
into mad realms

gagaku

friends keep
        dying
making this poetry
seem rather
     useless

the demons
wearing black
     of course
       waving small wooden sticks
          with triangular white
            cloth
  little white flags
curve past me
held by black masters
      of death

the rainbow seems to be
     myself
tucked away
behind this
     typewriter

so many friends are dying
     spirits never
 to pop up again
from behind a building
        from
under a pier

at my old front door
so many compatriots
     gone

as they go a part of me joins each
        a piece of this
soul

I'm not one to be
           left totally alone

I tell you

the demons continue to weave
        past me
waving their little white flags

gagaku

this is where I 'get off'
I am not fool enough
to expect
fame and fortune

I am not fool enough
to be unsatisfied

with the little I have
I'm content

to beat off occasionally
fuck once in a while
for my honesty

upon you
will treat you better
than anything
of the same
or opposite sex

this may be difficult
to understand

yet the poem lasts
the beautiful coital experience
fades after a day
or two

GAGAKU

some of the best things are crooked
some of the deadliest
display perfect symmetry

I awake
try to think of a job
to perform

something useful
social
enjoyable

somewhat lucrative
who will hire me
with my seven arrests
who will
hire me with my felony burglary
        record
no one of course
I'll take care of the family estate
the only way to survive and
I'll write these poems
spread them over earth's surface
kick
the eyes of my readers
    in
their soul gut

I'll continue on
at least for the next
                5 minutes . . .
my job
is poetry.

this seat is comfortable
my chair of poetry
wicker
good for my back
demons are clapping for me here
big grey white cloth covered
hands clapping

                baudelaire was right
            the more I write
                each day
            the less I fornicate

    the body moves off
                        the soul my spirit is
                                here
        Baudelaire Lautreamont Rimbaud

    Lautreamont was right
        borrowed that currency
    from dad
        to pay for the first
                        Maldoror's print

    so much spirit
                he lost his body
                        entirely
            soon after
                        publication
        Rimbaud Baudelaire Lautreamont
        and
        Rimbaud stayed alive after his
                        spirit
            was put upon paper
                he moved off
        his body moved off
                        to gather currency
                        gun running?
            selling new ovens?

    he lived for cancer of that leg
        a sour reward

    Rimbaud Lautreamont Baudelaire

3 frenchmen
I adore.

❖

I
thought I was dying last night
that's how great the tightness
in my middle stomach was

Perhaps it was the woman
who visited me yesterday

she has a very jealous mate

He came to my door
like always
save when he parks
          in my crumbling
                    driveway
and honks for 15 minutes
while I suck
her

I'll have to
        change my way
Yet if I change
I'll be him waiting
outside my lover's
          mate's
cave

✧

There's no choice
we are the cuckolded
          or the cuckolder.
          do I misspell that?
The Demon says no.

He holds up a square white paper
facing it toward me
it is 18 inches square
the word NO is printed
in thick black lettering

Why should I receive my answer
          from the Demon?
The angel has no time
          for me
he is busy playing flying
about
          twirling in
clouds and peace
like a cherub
giggling and masturbating
          his small
harp.

❁

I like to relax
let the forms take their shape
red balls
black wires for hair
you may disagree
dripping whitish phallus
limp and hanging
        half bigger than nothing
and half less in size
than everything

I like to relax
even repeat myself
there's a woman on my mind
she won't go away

I love to relax
sit here in this
perfect wicker chair
write these poems
to gagaku music
let the forms
    take shape

this is my voice
no one speaks
this ancient rhythm

you may disagree
I have to relax
speak myself here
there is a woman
on my mind
she's turned my balls red

thick black wires coiled about
antennaes of my center

this is my voice
I often repeat myself
this is my voice.

✵

I've a fig tree
full of birds

just after fall
no leaves

they're here for the wild seed
I put out

I once killed a sparrow with a bb gun
when I was around 8

I still see it falling
straight down
about 25 feet down

from a limb
and now I've raised a thousand birds

demons clap for
me they applaud

standing about in groups
they look at each other

and rub shoulders
like a group of businessmen

they wear glasses
plaid suits

a group of real estate agents

96

these demons

still the birds are just ten feet from me
in the limbs of fig trees waiting
waiting for my seed.

❖

I was running my bulldozer from
the middle of California's northern border
                    the flat one
                        up there with oregon
down south I moved
            cutting this state longitudinally in half
                        down to Mexico
                you know the small flat border

I manslaughtered 4 million humans
mostly in that big valley
                    with all the fruit
                            and spick farmers
11 million dogs and cats
trillions of insects
you can bet I was after life
all of it
the slightest specks of vileness

and now I sit atop my machine
                looking over the river
                        at Mexicali

I'll leave Mexico alone
those people have something
            worth saving

I am sitting 11000 feet up
          right next to lake mildred
                    high sierras
            a small fire cooking trout
               snyder off to side
    50 feet away
            huddled
      using small boulder for table
                    using twig for pen
                      dipping it in
            bottle of blood ink
      he secreted in his backpack

  writing that perfect cold mountain poem
      odd
I watch him work
            never knew he wet his pants
                      each time

✧

        I'll be alright
    as soon as I get
        to the typewriter

    it's all healed now
    I am here

    I am King here
  I'm young and strong
    bright & lucid

    the
  demons bow before me
raise & lower their bodies
    from kneeling position
touch their witch &
  warlock noses to ground
    three times

 here
  I am in control
you can only follow
    me with
  your eyes

 here
I dance
 down
 the
page

100

✪

windy morning
moon just into gemini
if you believe
hokus pocus

all that must be reckoned with
says my only father

I am inside the void
black space
some white around
splotches of it
      square shaped or rectangles of
            white round dots of white
    purple is about
        red
    yellow
    all the colors even mixtures
a goat
eating green grass
    nibbling yellowish teeth
    sort of a constant smirk smile
blue sky behind him
    or her
hope you don't mind
        I'm in the void
      can describe what I see
        inside

PAIR

he works at the local
   'free thinking radio
station

he runs poetry readings
for junior
   high school students

he talks so quickly
         you can't understand
him

he's trying to be something
     very quickly
   he is running
he can't be understood

his friend who runs at his side
    is too fat
  his heart gives out
he acquires the tic

the tic and the talker who
       can't be understood
   a literary pair

they're scratching their nails down my body
        down my ribs
      down my stomach
down my back
they are not above my nipples
  something keeps them below my chest
they've my balls cupped in their palms
they've my toes each grasped in
                one of their hands
they hold my knees
scratch my calves
I am total red beneath my chest
I feel no pain
I continue to create
I continue to live

❖

chase the poor animal away
walk to the night window
tap on it
he might be satan.

rub my right eye
take inhale of marlboro
continue this work
it is better than fucking
at this moment:

I sound this alarm:
demons above below at sides
everywhere omnipresent
swimming about me.

✪

I held her in my arms
    and she held me
      in hers and
      we did kiss
        and I did feel perfect

there are an endless column of white
      sheeted demons
         receding off into darkness
          or infinity

all their pink puds
        stick out from the front of their gowns
        though
      no hole in the gowns is visible
    a seamless sheet
      worn by each
  velvet or cotton not wool

each penis comes its whitish liquid cream
  there is blood in it
      long thin and some short
        lines of blood

I can't be perfect in telling you what I see
    white sheeted demons
        with pink dog peckers
        short
        upright things
        coming

✧

I had something right about last week
was making love every morning

this week may differ
there's a fish tank next to this typewriter
5 large angels study me

3 black 1 white 1 mixed stripe

this world goes on
who wants peace with death constantly near

hanglide
trapeze
tame the tigers
jet fly
etc

taunt death
excite her

the demons circle
all that black cloth
with a deep red glow

they circle

❖

understand
this is my horror
I have to create a torture
unreached by genet
                lautreamont
                artaud
                sade
                rimbaud
                any of the
                others
        to succeed

        it is demons
        who allow me the chance
        and God
        who oversees this combat

        an example:
        I cough them out of my jaw
        yellow robed creatures
            4 to 6 inches high

            like spitting a tornado
                        of black
                    I spit demons into
                the air
        hell out of my mouth
    a typewriter that works
        a mouthful of shit

❖

I believe we are surrounded by enemies
I believe San Francisco is a dead city
I believe New York is unkempt and in need of nourishing
I believe in witchcraft
when it is sleeping next to me
        dagger in purse

MAD ART

              my mother & father
are 2 of my
       best friends
       is this a crime?

GAGAKU

when it is working
each poem is a breath

he can relax this morning
his work is finished
he wrote 40,000 mediocre poems
one small tree
used up under his fingers

the cat danced to left and to
right outside the window
as he wrote
2 feet in front of his body

not a muscle in his body
left save in his
2 index fingers

he can relax now
smoke his cigarette
slowly

LIFEWORK

you just write
your
      fucking
poems
put'em in an envelope
and
send'em to the publishers

nothin else works
not being a
dealer
a actor swordfishboat captain
lawyer shopkeeper
musician prose writer
m.d. publisher
candle maker jewelry
nothin else works

you just write
those poems stick
them in an envelope
and send'em to
      the
publishers.

GAGAKU

they run up and back getting
smaller and larger

larger as they run up
smaller as they move back

light blue satin
robes

like nightgowns your
woman might wear

nice to the touch
a smooth shining material
perhaps silk

they are my violence
here I bleed them off

were I to discontinue
this exorcising process

I am confident
actual murder would be

part of my bio.

GAGAKU

peace
in the morning
a neat colorful home
3 dogs out front
wonderful ancient music
old men singing right from th'core
all the demons and angels embrace
hump themselves to butter
with holiness & sin
the angels don't fuck
have no erection
no wet vaginas
believe they are merely
hugging

the demons have large green
purple red scarlet orange
yellow white
black grey blue
    cocks

what a scene
only for my eye
and now

for yours.

GAGAKU

so this is how we beat death
play bongos in the black night of a beach
                come to this typewriter
                see a kite
                  follow its string down
                to earth
  count 3 claws holding it
          long nails
  definitely evil
try to describe the monster
    try to portray our murder
try to actualize evil's root
it's all there before my eye
    blurred
it is my work to clear it
          make precise what makes
                negation

circling my head
black fluid snakelike
            weaving
                         through air
they circle my head

feign entrance into my ears

they don't get in.

this work makes me strong
pushes them away

my spirit my defense

GAGAKU

they're twirling their whip
at cows or humans

long black shining whip
with pink forked tip

there are many of them
yet there is only one whip

they all hold the whip
at one-foot intervals

there are rabbits too
along with humans and cows

I see a giraffe
elephant several dogs

their teeth show
their mouths locked in smile

or a gleeful grimace
very ugly creatures

the victims are all much better looking
but the demons

hold the whip.

GAGAKU

I scratch my left chest
  feels good
I put the marlboro into ashtray
  begin typing
here on this olympia

I hesitate
hesitate again

lift marlboro to my mouth
    inhale
put it back in ashtray

type some more
hesitate

and take another puff
hesitate once more

listen to the old men singing gagaku
listen to the phoenix

wild wild music

GAGAKU

so many people ask me
what gagaku is

I tell them
but they soon forget

it is shinto music
nothing more

I hear it on my phonograph
and I write poems to it
and to honor it
I title whatever poems I
write to it

gagaku

in america

no one
must be more
thick skinned
than the writer
unknown and obscure
who spends most of his
or her
time writing
or dreaming about
images for
poems
and lets the hours
that could have been
spent making
a buck another way
slide away
in favor of
the written
art
mother will scream
papa will say it's
a mountain of playing cards
balanced on each other
so fragile so easy
to fall
useless to the
card table
without rewards

others will simply
call this writer
crazy

and keep away

from him or her

no one
must be more
thick skinned
than the writer
obscure and unknown
at least around here
in america

this morning

I awoke
about 4:30
read an hour of Graves
liked it and him
now it's still dark
but the sunrise
will be in
about half an hour
I've a huge tumba drum
and if I'm lucky
I'll take it out on the jetty
1 mile south on the
beach
and beat to the
sun rising
I've done it
more than 150 mornings
always a high
great exercise
pelicans come listen
seagulls circle
the pacific beats up on the rocks
on both sides of my perch
I love it
several times a woman has appeared
danced to my rhythm

gagaku

it's what
he has mastered

the writing
the description
the envisioning
the seeing
of demons

it's crazy
sure it's
foolish

but there's method
to his
art

he feels it's exorcism
therapy
helps him more than
any shrink
and some of his
work
actually gets
published
printed
in poetry
magazines

he believes
if he can see
a few
even a crowd
perhaps only a single

demon
it brings the monster
from within him to
outside him
upon his
poetry page

he sees the thing
or things
dancing and black robed
with multicolor sash about
their waists
he sees them smile
now grimace
now weep
a kind of mock
weeping

well

you gotta go against the best
and you might as well write it
than mumble it to yourself
vocally
I go against the best
for me
I go against Bukowski
it's what I measure my work against
and his always comes out better
no one else
comes even close to me
and sometimes I'm dishonest enough
with myself
to believe that I come close
to him
maybe I do now and then
you gotta go against the best

alone

I can't look the man in the eye
the doctor
I had to keep looking
away
oh I'd return to his eye for
3 seconds a time
but I couldn't make it
longer

misanthrope is the word
fits my soul

self-pity by the ton

my readers come to visit me
but don't like the look
of my cottage
and drive away

ginger bread home

I'm glad they leave
I've a single lily plant in my garden
planted it myself

wouldn't want them to step
upon it

with eye or boot

gagaku

what good does it do?
drive a lincoln?
go to tahiti?
swing a bullock by
its stout neck?
write a poem?
tap tap here on this
electric noisy machine?
hear birds singing?
that does some good
I like that part
I hear them singing
I put some wild bird seed
out for them to eat
just 5 minutes ago
that does some good
good for my ego my
I
I'm proud of that
It's almost better for me
than the birds
still I hear them singing
it's more for me
you know

how

do you fight
a guy like henry?
you don't
you stay out
of his way

he writes
too well
well enough
to grab
your woman

well enough
to make
you quit your own
art

let him
write the great
poems of this
modern world
he says it
so much
better

how to
fight him?
you don't
stay away
cash his letters
in

the collectors
pay large

sums for his signature
and notes

how do you
fight henry?

nada

he's a junkie
issuing a call for help
everybody hears
but nobody comes

what he really wants
is just a small amount
of junk each day
legal and without fear

no way
not from this alcoholic
system
nada

oh he likes a beer
once or twice
a week
and a joint now and
again

but basically
he's an opium junkie
issuing a call for
aid

everybody hears
nobody comes

gagaku

it is
a fine place
for a poet to
be
in a jail
being called
asshole by
a narc

I
was there
just 4 hours
seemed like 4
years
at the time

bad time
I've no wish
to return
such choices I'm
perhaps
presented

I remember
what I said
in jail
it's God's will
I said

not an atheist
for 4 hours

not booked
they let me go

saved me
money
for bondsman
    lawyer
    etc

the demons?
I saw no demons
in jail

It's

now time to
write a
modern
poem—no rhyme

I've no inspiration
in me
but I'm about
to be fired
from my present
caretaker job and
have to make
a living
so it's poetry
writing I've
chosen for
a new
vocation

art?
to hell with
art. I've got
to pay my
rent and utilities
medical and insane
insurance premiums

this the other that
expense
is the reason for
this poem

you
say no

one will pay?

Bah—I havn't lost
my job yet
still have my drum unhocked
a color t.v. and
auto too

point

      well I've
     never got
   along with
     women
or men and that
  is the reason
  I get along best
    with publishers
           I've
         never and
     never will
      meet

this woman that was just here
              she left in a
         'huff
   not 4 minutes
  ago after
    she read
my new poem stack

      wherein
    one of the poems
     I seemed to have
    stated the line
I know no women
      just girls
  this

seemed to upset
    her to the
    point of
   leaving rather
     than loving

135

which as I
　　told her as she
got into
　　her mercedes
　　　in a 'huff

you're
proving
my point.

he

drugged himself
then wrote poems
by the dozen

he
tried all kinds
of new meters
fiddled with the
typewriter's marginal
apparatus

he
was a fiend for
    originality

he
was one of
thousands who
opiated themselves
or drank vino
pot
pills and then
wrote

poems
poems by the kilo
it gave him a measure
of self respect

helped him and the
thousands
like him live another
day feeling they

and he were
more than
a mere 186 pounds
of garbage

gagaku

              way out of balance
         way off center
              that's this
                   poet
right now

bitter bitter poison
         I'm down
      on the human

   I stay
         alive more
                for the animal
   sky clouds
         ocean motion

      the human
      I included
   I'm way down on it

      she appears
               tells me she'll
                  be my muse

tells me she'll be seen with me
               often in public
                     if I get
                        an old mercedes

         and she's
               a good poet
         supped upon wormwood

and she's a wonderful fuck

139

              supped upon me
        and I her

and what
              has an
        old mercedes
        to do with
           anything?

2.

he writes the way he
wishes

gagaku

someday when my courage is up
I'll write a flock of poems
without ever reading them

I'll send them to an editor
with a little forenote
asking him
or her to fix any obvious
typos

I won't make copies
nothing is more enjoyable than receiving a magazine
with my work in it
that I have never read before

then it really tells me something
about myself
and if such a poem or poems
are actually good
they'll tell me even more than
merely something about
myself

but hell
I'm just fantasizing
I've never done th'above
I edit over and over
chop stanzas and add them
make sure every word is spelled properly

once the editor of the defunct "Open City"
underground newspaper in LA
changed a word of one of my accepted poems
he changed *like* to *kike*

and he knew I'd been raised a
jew

that's when Bukowski wrote an hysterical satire of that
editor—that satire was printed in an evergreen review
with a huge circulation - that editor was torn to his gut
by Bukowski's story - I'll always believe that was Bukowski's
way of helping me out

but hell
maybe I'm just fantasizing
it's 12-6-83 and Bukowski is still my president of america
he thinks I don't like him anymore and I think he doesn't
like me anymore
bah
I'm just fantasizing

prospects

I just
  don't know
      how I'm
    going to
  find the
    right woman

certainly
  not at nagasaki
massage down
    the block
    though
        koko touches me
            just right
            and always
        helps me on
          with my jacket
                after rubbing
              me down with
                a hot wash rag

apparently I'm harmless here
just a little man
on a porch
next to santa monica
beach
typing

so they let me be with their
1st amendment

I don't have any overwhelming plans
for the political system
so they
let me be

I avoid the cops and I avoid you
I don't avoid the
wild birds   my cat
save occasionally

or the muses
the muses avoid me
much of the time

I would rather the muses
be here all the time
lower lips spread

rosey flesh radiating

graceful animals
with marble warm skin

I'd treat them better than
myself

wouldn't allow them to smoke drink any
of my liquor

I'd feed them lettuce and meat
rub their backs with hot soapy rags

rub their flesh with rose cream
why aren't they here

ehhh they're out farting in some other
artist's nostril

the ones on the best seller list
in art week magazine

that's where the muses are

gagaku

I've tried much
come back to poetry writing
will stay
I'll take intermissions
enough not to stale myself

I've tried oil painting
sold a few
and I'll go back to it
during intermissions

but my serious
effort
will be this
demon seeing

I light a cigarette
seeing demons is something
no one does as well as I
in poetry

no one else
even tries

silver and gold gowns
sparkling
glittering

they move
slowly
and speed up
jiggling about

they wear cowboy boots

bullets in a belt
around their now
black and grey gowns
robes

I take another puff

I'm not going to quit
until I'm dead
it's true
it holds me stronger than any
wife

gagaku

I'm typing my poems
on lighter weight paper
now
the postal rates
have climbed
as you know

I'm writing my poems
and in them
talking
to you to
myself when I
re-read them

I'm seeing demons in my
poems now
I have enough confidence
in my imagination to
know I can see demons
here

they have not
shown up
yet but I know
they're coming

a sexual image involving
demons comes to me
but is too
profane to relate
just 19 seconds
ago a songbird outside
my cottage
hit a trill that can

not go unmentioned

the demons wave silver trays
coins jangle the tray
gold coins silver
coins
nuggets of
silver and
gold

gagaku

                    I'd travel but I can't
                    afford it
                    I haven't sent stories to hustler
                and got that 1500$
            for a trip to germany
                    or france
            but there's plenty here
                to describe

            I remember germany
                pigs spitting in parks
                    I remember tangier
            swollen ankles big as my chest
goiters like honeydews hanging
            from necks

        I remember italy
            musty
        the slums of genoa
            equal to harlem

I remember monaco
    sparkling false diamonds
and nice that beach of rocks
    and valencia the
                best paella in this
                world

gagaku

this is the first poem
perhaps for 8 months

it has little chance to
succeed

it's going to wormwood review for
judgment

and now its time to
get down to
biziness

I did paint 50 or so
canvases in the
silence of
the last 8 months

but the hell with that
it's time to get
down to buziness

demons in burlap
bags
potato sacks
only eyes show through
holes in the
sack

and there's not much
to see

the whites of the iris
are more

                    grey than white
            large black pupils
                now reduced to pinpoints of
            black

the mouth seems to be moving
            under the sack
        large lips seem to chew slowly
                    as a camel

        perhaps it's not the
                    stuff of art
                this camel like chewing
                    of lips under
                    burlap

the last reading

I'm going through
hundreds of old poems
most back from editors
rejected over and over
something made me keep
them about

but today is the last
reading
if they don't show
at least a bit
of art

into the fireplace
they'll go

gagaku

I was sent to clean out a dead woman's apartment
   there was a manuscript
      various "spiritual" writings
      she had been struck on the yogi brahmins
         gurus from india
   and this was not my type
   of writing
            she died old and mad
            first screaming profanity
         at her neighbors
   before passing away

            now the manuscript
      gathers dust in a garage
      I showed it to a fellow writer
   and he said no like first I'd said no
         but something
      keeps me from throwing
      it totally out

      she has no
   relatives for me to
      pass it to

               maybe she was
         a van gogh like genius
      and my shallow eye can't
         pick it up
   oh impossible!
               yet let some other human
         judge it when he cleans
   out the garage
         after my old mad
         Death

gagaku

I like it more
    when my lines
                move about the page

            I like it more
            without a clear
left hand margin

        a sense of freedom
    at least to my own eye
    is expressed

    sometimes
one of my poems
        that have a freedom of
    motion on the page
looks to my purposely blurred eye
            like a thing
                dancing
    perhaps balancing on one
            foot
    in the midst of a step

sometimes
    the profile of one of my
                        poems looks like the
side of a monster's face
    teeth protruding

a demon

gagaku

I think I've lost it
the ability
to write poems

I still
see demons

round faces
fisheyes
moist and bulbing

thinning hair on their tophead
ties on
over scaled suit

long pointed fingernails
more like talons

regular human flesh on hands
rings worn
shining
ruby large red radiant ruby
held in a silver
setting
on one little
talon

they twirl their sex organs around
twirling penis like a yo yo
swung about in
a perfect circle

I think I've lost it
the ability

to care
live
love and write
poems

horns on the top of their head
two goat like horns
coming out of
up from that
bald rather
almost bald
head

gagaku

       maybe I'll write a poem
          that works

      maybe I'll describe a demon
         that a reader
    will see

       maybe I'll end my life today
         though
      the demons would be very
        upset

      no
I'm here to describe them
   I know
I've said that before

     they have grey rabbit ears
        white fur on the inside
           and pink flesh holes

     ants crawled inside the ears
       and inside the eyes
          of my dead human friend

       That's what his wife said
        she found him inside his little
     boat

just three blocks from here
     he swallowed a liquid glass
         of phencyclidine
       misspelled?

160

he did he did
angel dust
he chose his death

rocketed right through
I respect that

yes
the demons laugh and clap

gagaku

I have not written
        rather I
            have not sent poems
                to publishers
                for a year

            but I have written

much

I have read too
        conrad mencken james
        mann havelock ellis
                the wormwood poets too

alos rather also usually the morning
                paper

        I value reading as much as
                        poem writing
                            or playing a
                                conga drum
                                    or quinto or tumba
                                drum

        or oil painting or drawing
            or putting together
            a poetry magazine
            or prose
                prose I like too

        I like it all I
            am almost a happy man

and there is the
                fig tree out front
                I look see at it
                    and feel it is
                    not time to move

            such it has been for 20 years
            in this place

here the grass is still
                greener

        when
        I want
        time to fly
I paint

l a

I
would rather
write badly and have fun
than write well and be miserable

I would rather see my words here
swell out like a growing organ

yesterday I completed a prose novel by john fante
ask the dust fante breathed new spirit into me and I was
gleaming and healthy mad trotting
about my house
all day and even now

I'm full of the life of that
wonderful book

it is the definitive los angeles novel
I know
I was raised at
alvarado and temple

gagaku

I didn't have to scrape
              for the royalties
                        I had a
                                  grandmother
                        who left some property
        to manage

        raise the rent
                        call a plumber
              fix a broken
                        pane
        lower the rent
                   the tenant can't
                             afford a raise
                             with his
                             mercedes
                                  tucked in
                                       a hidden

              garage

        I didn't have to scrape for the royalties
                        you can have
                             them cherrycoughski

        write bukowski's biography
                        ferlinghetti's
royalties! get them
        be a figure!

I'll take the demons sitting round
                        a wood table
                   well stained
        I'll take them beating talons
              on the top

fangs wet for teeth
                white grey & yellow
        changing colors
that's what I'll describe
            keep your
                    royalties

    nobody rings my phone except a loving hooker
      wondrous blessing!
no fans at the door heaven sent blessing!
    I've got the solitude
                had
                    it for years
    damn good day
        the demons agree put their
                        arms around each
                                other
                        a big group hug

GAGAKU

the girl here
a few weeks ago
is 33 years old
keeps a dagger tied to her ankle
as she makes her way about
southern California
streets
served as a focus of female dedication upon the page
of one of my chapbooks
was first plugged by me in 1973
this is 1983
I used to tell her I loved her and I did love her but
this time around she asked me to buy her dope so many times
nagged so often that I stopped loving
her
she told me how she had to stab some fellow in the back
back at her family home in boise
he was about to rape her . . forced his way in
"foot in the door"
    ehh shit
        demons shit right before my
       imagination
now wipe themselves
with pale blue "soft" toilet paper
     now stab each other in heart
a green and yellow blood drips
over their nipples
they have the chests of young men
    rather hairless
     and they laugh and weep simultaneously
    as they stab
I drove this girl up to see her husband
he's always in jail
   some corrections camp in the malibu hills

he's working fire detail
        clearing brush
    at a dollar ten a day
he's never looked so well
when he gets out of jail in a month or so he'll hit the venice streets hustling
heroin and in a few months
he'll be down to bones again
on the streets, a free man, he stops eating—
only in jail does he exercise, eat
I've seen this happen five times—
2 years in jail—4 months on streets—3 years in jail—
9 months on streets—
the girl tells me they have a successful relationship
because he's almost always in jail

IT COULD BE

Artaud was right
about opium being absent from
our human bodies
by some mistake that occurred
hundreds
or thousands of years ago

and if he was correct
it would explain why the old man—
my neighbor across the street
just told me
"Boy you're really getting fit"
when I walked by him 2 minutes ago
on the way to my shack

I had an undershirt on and
he figured I should be "freezing to death"
as he put it
but I was actually quite warm
after all the sun was out
and bright—
it wasn't any less than 50 degrees

"chemistry" I told him
meaning the methadone I gulp each morning

I didn't tell him that though
I just said "chemistry"

he's an old beer drinker
I see empty cans by the dozen
out on his curb
every garbage pickup day

and old beer drinkers apparently get
cold

the only time I get cold is when I'm not
on an opiate
then 95 degrees in my shack
still doesn't warm me

it could be
Artaud was correct
no doubt they cut him off of opiates at
Rodez
maybe it's that that killed him

Kafka had to plead for morphine
for months before they would give him a shot
finally on the day before his TB death
"much better" Kafka said

it amazes me what sadists some doctors
are

WHEN HE GETS WORRIED ABOUT HIMSELF

he
goes to his typewriter and works
then he is
worried about himself
      but working too
and a busy bee
  according to william blake
has no time
   for sorrow
so if blake was right
he will worry without
     sorrow
which is
 something

GAGAKU

    lots of demons seated
in audience clapping
   at a poetry reading

    ferlinghetti up on stage
      bows and waves
        his russian type
     fur hat
   falls off
he picks it up

he has a beard
     which he scratches now
  staring at the crowd

he looks incredulously at the crowd
    as if he's unsure that
      they are there
        or real

    that is why
I don't read poetry
   anymore in
  public

GAGAKU

I don't know where to go from here
I could see demons
juggling apricots and
cooking pans
and green seedless grapes

I could take a walk along main street
in santa monica
and watch boxers work out
down at joe louis's gym
3 blocks away

but I did that
2 hours ago

also I watched 12 women move
in one of those exercise studios
that dot almost every city block
in current america
nov. 17, 1983

those women have an exercise leader
who gives forth with expert body motions
and barks
like a seal
or puppy bitch

barks orders
and the 12 females
follow those ordering barks
better than any order
I'd ever
give

THE GOOD

days I get poems
 accepted
   the bad days
   I get poems rejected

             today
          is a bad day
       I need a drink
    I'm going now

        to the cupboard
        if I remember correctly
        ahhh half a half
         pint of

        popov
   I'm not a drinker
        I'm a joint or 2 a day
     man and

a methadone dose each
                morning man
   ohh shit that tastes

   good—
       warm down my throat
               right now hitting my
                  inner tummy

           delicious

JACK

Jack looked to his right
at all those typed pages of crap
maybe there was something good in there
but Jack was too sick of them to
go back and read himself again
he was sick of his own prose and poems
he was sick of all humans except his old man
who was sick and dying at kaiser hospital
maybe the old man would make it for
like he himself said "another few years"
ehh shit
the streets were the same
the bukowski books were piled high
in every bookstore
it didn't make a difference
the place was fucked
this place
earth
fucked
there was just a new class of rich
and they didn't want to change
Jack thought of his 1500 in the bank
and savings and loan
two different accounts
Jack didn't want to change
he only hoped some of those women
he had known
would be back
none of them had been back
for over a year
and all he had
was his miserable fucking poems
and prose
he'd send them out

and they'd get picked up
here and there
and each time was a victory for Jack
he was talking
he was talking to human beings
through his art
he told himself THAT
was all that mattered
but
he really
missed those
ladies of the night.

MONKEYFACE REMEMBERS

there
is no mail
today
it's vet day
but still I keep looking out the window at my mailbox
hoping to see mail

I forget every several minutes
that there is no mail today

something
must be wrong with me

what is a writer without mail?
bukowski thought I might be wigged out.. a wolf
on his track
pleasants told me I was cruel
ruby called me cold and
stupid
marissha said I was stingy and self centered
a professor told me I stood upon a soapbox
in my poetry
a lawyer called me a conflicter of interest
and a mismanager
a cop called me amoral and
an
asshole
a poetess wrote of me as a reptile
and a critic said I copied william carlos williams style
a kid in grammar school called me monkeyface
over a hundred times
a young woman I thought might be aphrodite
called me arrogant insightful honest and self
indulgent

and implied my attempts at "love" were
            awkward
the girl who lived next door screamed that I was a
god damned motherfucking asshole a week
before she overdosed on coke
and valium
and
alcohol

and
there's no mail today

I'll recover

FINALLY

the drug addict
doesn't get "high"
  anymore

  ingests more & more
with decreasing intoxication

gains a "tolerance"
for the toxic
drug

then it is
he
or she is most
in danger of overdose
death

because when asked
he
or she will say
"I didn't feel high
so I hit another
bag on top
of the other
two"

this after the cops
and the
fire dept. rescue team
have just barely
saved his
or her
life

the fact is I knew personally
and well Mike, Alfred, Jerome, Tim, Jim,
Venice, Marta, Marlene
and just as acquaintances 8
other dead folks

all before the age of
33
gone from drugs
"nipped in the bud"
american citizens

so reader be
    careful

no

        I don't want to write a gagaku poem now
no way
    let the demons rest
     deep
or maybe shallow in my imagination

       I don't want to see them
         and write about them
      I'm sick of 'em.
there one is now waving at me
      it looks like the girl staying with me

      that little lovable wave
     she's gotta get out and wave her ass
they all got to get out and wave their ass

     can't lock'em in a cage
      why
    even I gotta get out and shake my ass
        once in a while

      hm hm hm hm
          I laugh this little
     ugly laugh to myself as I write
   and I don't like my
    little ugly laugh to myself
so I shut my mouth
     then I whisper to myself
           "so I shut my mouth"

     and it sounds
        much better

gagaku

why does he live with the woman
if he writes
about her
in a negative
fucking shitty fashion?
I mean
she's in the other room
trying to write
and she is a fool
she's not making it
not making grand art
and he lays on his bed
and he knows she
is all wrong
haywire
and he writes his poem
about how
erroneous her
attempts views and
between the lines
he is telling us
her soul is
a misconstruct

yes
his poem makes it
he gets his point over
to us
it is fine art
it sells
his books go well
his audience

is new huge

is that why he has her around?

what is going on

I put this paper in the typing machine
to send a small letter off
to a mag that
accepted 2
poems

glad
I was going to say
glad a couple worked for you
appreciate it
it's the first stack of submissions I've
sent out in several years

I was
going to write
but I don't see any real reason for it
the editor took 2 out of 20
I'm batting 100

it's not good enough
why should I phony glad hand the editor
he's got mms coming in from thousands
of hearts-souls
and he sends 99% back
unaccepted

I should be happy I'm batting a hundred
but I'm not

I want to hit 800
have the sucker print 16 out of the
batch of 20

I'm tired of this

minor leage shit
league that is

if I'm ever to get away from the
domination
of my bosses
I need to make a living at
my writings
how do you just get out there and
grab a following?

I don't know how and
being in the great majority is
very little consolation
so many of my friends
overdosed
gone dead buried through

the hell if I know
what's going
on.

gagaku

that's it
no more poems this morning
the methadone is coming on
and I want to lay back and enjoy it
the demons are both nodding to me and shaking
their face side to side
making the 'no' gesture

I'll get no straight answers from them
this time I didn't even ask them a question
and still they're giving me those
face moves

yes no yes
no

the serious artist

fills mountains of paper with shit and he's a fuckhead I know
I meet him everyday and he can't write either you bet I know

he doesn't stop either at one stanza he may ponder it a while
but he'll go on make 2 and he's a jew and he hates absolutely
hates you and doesn't care it's known he doesn't care and is dull
and always alone because no one can stomach him and only
            dope
allows himself to take himself for another day at his beloved
antique smith-corona

is usually bitter amazed the bombs havn't already dropped
what's holding those fuckers from doing it?   They're all so
poised and well paid and professional you'd think they would
want to get it over with is this to go through infinity?

thugs the politicians are thugs
  the russians the americans
chinese all those thug politicians
murdering in their fucking wealthy way while
millions of ... eh
what's the use

millions of serious artists
there are millions of serious artists

gagaku

it's not fair what I do
it's privileged information that I steal
and set down here
for your eye
and my eye later
when some good human
sees fit to
publish this

good humans publish
bad humans write
I write
sometimes I publish but very little
sometimes I'm good but very little
hardly at all
trust me
stay away
my life isn't so bad
with you away
I'm almost- always alone now
oh
I need other humans about
me at times

as for a wife & kids?
I don't know what it is like

I had a wife
but I left her
weeping for me
not to go

I felt something in me wouldn't survive
if I stayed

something in me was being killed off
not by her
but by the relationship

it was simply a matter
of getting enough
oxygen

the relationship made it almost impossible
for me to breathe naturally

that was 20 years ago
of course I made the right decision
she agrees now
and do you know we had some fine fucks
12 years ago

ahh

it's a wonderful night
a wonderful wonderful night
I was in the bar area
of this ocean park's most popular
restaurant
"the famous fish company"
and the bar was packed with
beautiful blond
girls and
gorgeous brunette girls and
I ordered a bowl of white chowder
it was superb
the bar so packed and everybody
save me
so serious about their alcohol drinks
I didn't recognize 2/3 of the drinks asked for
such imaginative names
way beyond this literary fool
and the girls
they were so beautiful
I can't get over them
I felt so good being around them.
and having them sneak peeks at me
I ordered another white chowder and
the bartender was grand
he refilled my ice water
without any request at all
it was sublime
and I looked at the girls
and sipped my soup
I don't think anybody was having as good a time as I
they were so serious about their alcohol
nobody could be that serious and truly
enjoy themself

so I left a buck tip
the bartender liked that
he knocked the bar in front of
me twice with his knuckles
to show thanks
I was proud
all the girls saw it
they all loved me
I could tell as I strode out
ready for methadone
once more
tomorrow morning

Thursday

hell
things aren't so bad,
I sent a postcard
to a lady
(who fucked me over)
Monday
and I shook as I wrote
supposed jest.
One woman in the world
        makes me nervous

now all the lines above
were written
ten years ago
today
things are terrible,
I spend all my money
almost all
on ———, and I'm
        weak

I still love that woman
in the first stanza
but I have not seen
her since 1977
and I've crossed out her
new phone number and
address
before I could memorize
        them

so that I
won't pester her
ever again.

there has got to be
some kind of goddam
honesty
or we might as well
be selling used cars

wanda

was often worrying
about her hair

I met her while
closing my gate

she was in her car and had stopped
at my driveway

to ask me if there were vacant
pads nearby

I told her my back room
was empty

as soon as 1 saw her face in her car
I wanted her not her car

in the shallow sexual sense
I achieved the fulfilling of this desire

but I had to as a pre condition
move a two car garage's contents

packed to its ceiling
with boxes of all sorts of flotsam

every conceivable item in the world no
rational person would save

I had to move it.all to another garage
                14 miles away

and also put in a washer and dryer at my shack

to achieve my desire

we made love 3 or 4 times
          maybe even 5 but no more

she was after a rich producer in the marina
                    del rey
     and I was her stepping stone
          I knew it and I played my role
                    perfectly
                    no pain
          now she is happily married to her man and
               they have had 2 sets of
               twins

my only rule for her was no
          men allowed in my
               cave

he

was amazed
he survived
so long
(decade) with only
art for a shrink

art kept him
centered enough
to survive

he had a myriad of faults
ranging from heavy narcotics
to chain smoking

but he knew enough
to go to art
when real danger was
just an inch away

art pushed the danger
away knowing danger
would finally
win but still
respite was acquired

he stuck to art
as most humans stick
to God
in fact he equated
art with God

art was God
for him
earlier in his life

he had centered himself
about woman

during this period he
cane down with
malignant melanoma
so he cast woman out
not totally out (a
few days here &
there allowed)

and turned to
art

the kid

  with the silver spoon in his mouth
hasn't found out
that silver spoons are hard
on kidneys

he has a different colored pair
of sweat pants for
    each emotion
red for boiling anger
purple for suppressed rage
blue for around the house
so

he misses the farts of a woman the
decibels of her closing
  after
        sex

he misses...everything except typewriter noise

what is it about poetry that grabbed him?
he doesn't know
  he burps
    and simply feels right
writing the
shit

"shit"-the word has become rotten
it's used too much

look at me
how desperate I am to screw a page

painting was much much quieter

almost silent

the girls seemed to like it better
one actually put her fingers on a wet canvas

and sought to excuse herself
  by sexing

the kid
the painter

he stops between stanzas and takes a big
inhale of marlboro

all the humans who used to bother him
are dead

he's actually truly really
alone now

gagaku

so many of these are published
I am a published poet
            who lives alone
            on santa monica beach
                        the ocean park section
        and
            demons look at me
        what are you going to write now? they seem
            to ask
        they want something about
                    jerking off
                now they hide their mouths with
                    their claws' palms
                            and whisper seemingly
                    to each other

            now they
                    jerk off
                        but I don't look
            too closely
        at this picture facet of my
                imagination

gagaku

       they carry various colored umbrellas
very pretty scene
one editor
    a woman
  told me she was
        worried about my "line breaks"

      what the
     f is a line break?
       is
  it when I write
  something like
    this:

     demons picking nostrils smiling
     acting disgusting
comical if not so
      ugly

ugly images for my
     imagination

  what's the

  good for
   anything?
  they're angry with me
I don't feel friendly with my demons
I feel "at odds" with them

   I have been keeping very distant from
        women
      emotionally

for about a
year

and it hasn't
harmed
us

I watch

the new books on santa monica's library
    shelves

Bukowski books
Creeley books

Ginsberg's thick new tome
I watch it

no one has ever checked
it out in the 9 months

it has
waited

it's too thick
too gaily heavy

the Bukowski books are usually
checked out

the Creeley like Ginsberg
never leaves

I don't check them out either
Gin & Cree

Buk's Ham On Rye I checked out
and read and

proclaimed it the best novel
in recent decades

but I'm opinionated and

prejudiced and never

preface my lines with
IN MY OPINION

or
I THINK

both Gin & Cree seem to me
condescending fellows

   I'm glad I've
never met either

as for Bukowski
his Ham On Rye

will
never spoil

yesterday

I smoked heroin and got a headache

2 weeks ago I smoked heroin and
mixed with pork ribs and methadone
I received insane stomach agony before
crapping a week's worth

I'm not a creature of taste
those who proclaim their taste
to me are rats

to trap a rat
one needs
peanut butter & honey

they are so
particular

I've had problems with rats in my life
one woman born in the year of the rat—1948

one rat I killed in my garage
with honey & peanut butter

the woman killed me but
I got the rat

the woman killed the candleshop in me
all she had to do was walk by my shop's
front with another fellow
a fellow who looked like a

faun

and then I
who hadn't written in two years
gave to that venice beach neighborhood
10000 bucks worth of free
                    candles

and went home to write thousands of
odes that irritate quite a few
                literary hustlers
me
I was born in th'dragon year
and I fell in love with a
                    rat

have you ever seen a dragon
                        waiting
                        for a rat?

```
W
O
W
```

the sun just came out
    around 9 a m
august 13

1986
and grey mornings have
        been our rule around here for
                weeks it seems

but now the sun
    and
the green fig tree leaves out my window
            and jasmine plant leaves
                plenty of sunlight vibrant green
                    I see it right now as I
                            type
                        through a bamboo shade

I erase an err above
(one you will never see)
with liquid paper

beethoven still on
        violins
            dancing on air
                    such order
                        such light yet unshallow
                            composition

I look to left and see tiny blue neon
                        tetras darting about
in mating procedure

5 of them
and I look for the little discus fish in there
        but he
        or she is
            hiding

hiding like I hide in this shack this
cave this
hideoug
      which is a
         typo I won't erase

sundays

          are best
      to lower shades and
              keep them down
       to stay in and write
     to hear the motors
       go by loud and
     competitive
              and to stay in
              and write and
              let them have
       the streets mashing each
                     other into
              vile soup

and now the sun sneaks
          through crack in bamboo shades
          and makes a
     zebra pattern upon this paper
          in machine and just
                     as quick is gone
              it's almost dark in here
              it is dark in here

          sundays are best to stay in and write
              this is the grandest victory
          known to me
              not a pool
              or ferrari
          or even a
          mate
       just this
              being here with me and staying
     in away from all of them

thank God

gagaku is not on
I'm beginning to despise gagaku music
it has shown me too many
demons

I bland it
or I blame it
gagaku
bringer of demons
to my imagery

I don't blame me
I can't
go around blaming
me

fuck the guilt
catholic women are always
always trying to
make me feel guilty
and often
succeeding

what do they have against a
reformed
jewish kid from
west hollywood
and now santa monica
but before west hollywood
central LA
or north central LA
temple & alvarado
rosemont elementary school
I threw up

40 times in a row on my entrance to
kindergarten
they changed the age back to 5 from 4 1/2
because of me
demons & retch
enemies
everybody is a goddam enemy of everybody else
and don't kid me with your
phony
    hug

gagaku

I don't like to re-read my poems
            I like to write them and send them
                and then read them when
they pass th'test
are published as
something decent decent
                    art

pound would call this shoddy but he
                        was scorpio
                            I aquarius we
                    are astro-enemies

demons twirl their aprons & paper
                    napkins
                as they dance
            in circle
        turn around so fast
                    a spin
I like to watch them dance
—humans who chose not to imagine
                    demons
                    are demons

the
catholic church
has imagination

when a man in those robes sprinkles water about a
                    coffin
        he has imagination

done

the mornings chore's
whoops that's wrong
the morning's chores
that's what I love about poetry
you don't have to be right
you can be left and make errors
just like that lady I saw down on Main Street
15 minutes ago
she has made lots of errors
I could tell
she walks up and down Main Street
seemingly 24 hours a day
she's all bruised and messed up
obvious alcoholic
I gave her a buck this morning
and she said, "thanks baby
I'll get something warm"
It's chilly and drizzling
a couple of weeks ago I yelled at her
"get the hell away from me"
but then I kept seeing her
on her 24 hour patrol
crookedly making it up
and down Main Street
poor fucking woman
poor fucking american woman
you go down to trendy Main Street
in the Ocean Park section of
Santa Monica
prosperous high fashion gourmet
Main Street
you'll see her
you won't be able to miss her

torn red knit cap
rags for clothes

gagaku

you see
I said
I thought there was a
robbery going on
I didn't know the 3 men at the
curb were two plain clothes
cops and one
 junkie
so I pulled away
fast
but 3 blocks later
I heard sirens everywhere
though not a police
car in sight

it's when I parked
they all of a sudden
(20 seconds)
were all around me
those 'robbers' had
sent my license plate
screaming through police
radios

as I was
handcuffed
in the back of one
I heard my name and
address
over 9 police radios
so loud so clear
so many citizen onlookers
wondering what all
the sirens were about

and me
the crook
caught
by santa monica mod squad
no
that's not true
black and white officers
neatly uniformed

lucky I wasn't holding
any dope
lucky I didn't plow into
that car as I floored it
through an alley
lucky I didn't wipe out a fine family
lucky I'm free
    tonight

gagaku

the jailors were both black
woman and man
the woman had a heart
she asked 3
or 4 times
what they were planning
for me
are they going to release
him? when?
she would say
as I peeked through
   bars

the male black
was fat and just
waved his arms
in silent
ignorance

for 4 hours I watched these two
joke with each other
corny and false hilarity
while 6 young mexican
junkies took their turn
to be booked

the 6 looked as if
each had been hiding in a
dark room alone
for years with only
a needle for a
companion
slumped and ill
      fed

skin bad
weak

finally she got a phonecall
that said release
me
they could have booked me
on reckless
driving they didn't

2

days after the chase
I'm out of jail
I talk with the guy
who accompanied me
in the car
and got away
before I got
handcuffed

he tells me
there were 3 guns
pointed at us
as I stepped
on the gas

I hadn't seen
the guns

had I seen the guns
I wouldn't have
throttled my car
away

good cops in santa
monica
they didn't blow the back
of my head away
I guess they knew
a brilliant poem
such as this

wouldn't have
made it

usually

each year
I get over to catalina island
for a day
and take my glass mask and a swim fin
out into the little bay
just south of where the
transport boats dock

this little bay
is a natural preserve
and fish abound
garibaldies
  calico bass
   a dozen other species
and some of those fish
  get 2
3 feet long

I buy a cheap loaf of bread
  and feed these fish
the water is perfectly clear
and once I show with the loaf
there are so many fish before my eye
they make up a solid blanket of glorious motion

  oh yes
take along a snorkel

well fcuk

can't even spell that right
walking the beach today
another err
today

fuck
suicidal
totally
and then a tiny bird on the beach walking
to my right side
he or she
between me and the ocean
a tiny white bird
one of those little santa monica beach birds whose feet
move
so fast
and she or he walked with me over 500 yards
stopping to rest when I
stopped
started just when I started
and it was just a single
little bird and
I had the
best
of company

life saving it was
took away my suicidal nonsense
feet so fast they blur
and then stopping when I stopped
and waiting for me
why?
something more than we know was with me when I
needed

x for unknown
        some call x God
              some nature
            some the muse of
                    poetry
no
    it was a little white bird
    who knew just as much and
probably more than I

aphroduckingdite

he was very close
        to her
        telling her
            how beautiful she
                    was and
                    she was very
                    close
            to something else
                telling him how
                rich she
                    wanted to
                    be

223

gagaku

wanton Aphrodite: I met her
                    made love to her
                    watched her eye other men
                    wanton she was
                    all she wanted with me was one night
                      why? my poetry

how do I know she was Venus?
her eyes changed from blue to green to brown

and I was sober
and it happened just that way
hell I must have spent 30 hours with her and
not one single characteristic
defies the truth that she was
I hope still is
Aphrodite
in person: I havn't seen her for 8 years
she's the only woman I extremely desired
who hasn't been by here on repeat visits

stole my wits: she did
stole my wits: and turned
              me into
          a full
        time poet
scribbling day after day
        year after year '
    of her absence: just over the hill
                      she's always just over the hill
                      coming home to
                      my arms

do you know what she told me?

"I'm just folks."

I didn't believe a word:
after seeing those orbs change color
from blue to green to brown

gagaku

I havn't taken
any days off from poetry writing
for the last several months

nor have I taken any days off
from feeding sparrows
finches and doves

and occasionally even seagulls
out on the beach
with stale rye or wheat
never white bread

the seagulls love stale bread
as well as fresh bread
I'm sure of this and
I'm sure of very few
      things

I could be wrong
I've been wrong before
when I was so very sure
I was right

gagaku

I was in love with the one who spent a night with me
I fell in love when I knew she would not grant me another
night praying at and on her body

and when I say pray I do
not mean prey

that was the apex of love making for me in my life
I know she was Venus

no doubt at all

demons in my unconscious come out to my conscious
and nod their heads affirmatively at me
they know too

nothing can be done about it
in my desire to get back with her I only
frightened her

I thought I knew all about women
but Venus does "steal the wits of the wisest of men"

no doubt at all

beating

the drum
the typewriter
the dirt out there
planting a dwarf orange tree
planting
many australian ferns or
asparagus ferns
I'm always mixing one for the other
some things I'll
never get right
never learn

        I will have spent the days of my life
                writing these poems
          this poem
        purely typical

now I've subscribed to a dozen small mags
all in their 1st
or 2nd issue
I want to see what they are saying
in today's
poems

the depth of revolution
        revulsion
how near it is to
        my little alamo
          by that pacific over there 127 yards

I'm writing poems just to hear the fucking sound of this
        typewriter
          it is all I have to tell me
         in real sound

                    true decibels
                    that I'm alive

there's no woman here
2 visit that are friends but
            what's friendship when one has
                    bedded aphrodite?

the memory of her is a curse--it was
                    so good it made all else
                    afterbirth

I want

all my readers to know
that at this very second
right now
as this poem is being written
approximately 8 2/3 blocks from where I am
now now
typing my poem
this poem
my underpants and socks are being dried
in a rickety old dryer
for 3 dimes

once I had a girl friend
     Wanda
and all was wonderful until I visited her
at a different laundry
only 3 blocks from where
my underpants and socks are
now drying

I said to Wanda, "Hi!" and kissed her
because she was so
       pretty
and she
said to me
"Goddamn motherfucking pissass—if you'd
hook up my old washer and dryer I wouldn't
             have to sit in this dump"

I was shocked
it was our first argument
   though I didn't really argue
           I just contacted Martin Plumbing
and had them hook up Wanda's old

                washer and dryer
both of which I transferred in U-Haul
            Truck from her
    previous San Fernando Valley place
                of residence
        to my shack on Santa
            Monica Beach

Wanda was very
pretty
and left me for a Hollywood Producer
        I was
                not heartbroken
now both the washer and dryer have broken down
so I put dirt in the washer and planted a quite
healthy fern—Wanda visits about once a year

we are in trouble

when friends
    actual friends
            offer to go on a heroin run
            for us

we say to him
            get the fuck out of here
            4 times in a row

        and finally he does
                we have better things for our money like
                chickensoup at zucky's deli
                        with rice and kreplach
        if that's how it's spelled

        1 day at a time says AA
        I drink alcohol sometimes
            splitting headache in morning
            but over by 11 a m
            no anyway
            I don't want any
                    fucking heroin

            it costs too much
        if it was free
    do you
want the truth?

gagaku

                last night
            first woman in 10 months
                a jap hooker
                    a little older
                        than most
                more relaxed the
                thing was I
                    had been reading
                    robert herrick and
            he mentioned
            buying the same sort
                    of
        grub
we need our god damn grub once in a while or we go
            plum stale

        and if it doesn't come to our
                front door and jump on us for
            our terrific artistic
                    talent
            then we must go to the store or turn
                plum stale

                    233

gagaku

this is freedom
I say this is freedom
I feel free
victoriously free
no dead ends for this
one
I'm free to see them waving american flags
up and down avenues they parade
proudly holding high american stars and stripes

they are girls in dallas cowboy cheer leader uniforms
breasts quite revealed
and bouncy
and demons in among them
and there's some of the football players too
in full uniform

today
I planted a dward orange tree
it had 4 or 5 little orange colored fruits
on it
I planted it in the most sunny place possible
out in the front yard

demons are laughing at me and they've got their fingers
in their mouths
they are sucking their own talons
now biting their talons as humans
bite fingernails

now they display their chewed talons to
one another
now they pick each other for fleas or ticks
or tics

english professors swing on each other
break each others glasses
in the race for fame
and tenure

rimbaud and lautreamont and baudelaire
were all english professors
they kept it a secret

not a dward
a dwarf

eh

they're all hunched over
    waiting to write an
        obit of me
        wanting to make me
        famous after my
                death

        like a little girl
told me once
an 18 year old with
        a fine body and
        frog eyes

    she said
        "you're going to be famous after
        you die"

and then she took off
                she wanted someone
                famous before he
                died

fame is having too many girls come
    and want to make love
            to you

fame is to
    go to bed with
        many of them
        and be impotent
        with most

fame is impossible to
            cope with

the cops are around
       the reporters are around
    seductive women
       are all over the place
wanting the famous one why? I don't know why

you know why
—I can just hear the reasons
   ticking out of your
forehead
that's a terrible image
but I can hear the reasons
        in your brain
does it have something to do with money? or nesting?
or ego? or security?

my parents

obviously do
not like
 my poetry

so I no longer
foist it upon
them

I keep my books to
myself
or give my free copies
to friends who
might understand and
appreciate

musicians
drunks
painters
junky women

they seem to like
my work
my parents do

not

gagaku

we leave him typing in his
lush shack by the sea
we leave him because all he writes of anymore
is demons
and there's more to life
than demons

there's trips to europe
and owning a BMW
and playing the horses

he should be playing the horses
instead of writing
of demons

he went to the track
but made the mistake
of going with a writer
the writer
scrambled here and there
just couldn't stay
in one place long enough
the writer
was a crazy dangerous fool

he plans to go to the track again
by himself
he has held it before him
like a gift he will
present to himself
a trip to the track
alone in the future

well

          the cafes don't open for an hour
     mozart is on the record player
and I can't go back to sleep
  I'm mad at this typewriter
    it skips
  I'm not made for
  typewriters that skip
      I am an improviser
  I'm made to horse
   shit here in the poem
and get away
   with it

I'm the free
  est poet there ever was
freer even than bukowski
  who's enslaved
rather enslaved by a left hand

          margin
        and his publisher
     who made him draw
    150 separate sheets
   for the
collectors

the secret of freedom is a legal private income
   that ought to make almost
    all my readers
    jealous
marlboro
cigarettes enslave me
opiates enslave me
aphrodite has no problem

whatsoever
   enslaving me
mozart sounds good
  he was born January 24th too
    just like me

when I told this to aphrodite she asked me
"oh are you mozart?"
  "no,"
I said,
"I'm Steve."

GAGAKU

I can afford to go "mad"
I have visa and master
chevron &
auto club
& Kaiser
medical credit card
I can afford to be a mad credit card carrying
    junkie poet
with 6000 in the
savings and loan
I can afford to have junkies
    real junkies put me down for my ultra
conservative use of the
drug they glutton

I can afford to be
honest on paper because
I've got my
bail money

GAGAKU

demons nod
their chins go up & down
saying
yes

women have given
up on me

an ugly came by and told me it would be nice
to have me in her mouth
    but
this disgusted me

I sent her off
now even she
doesn't visit

good
I can't do ugly women
especially when they tell me how
attractive
they are

GAGAKU

They look at me
eye me gaze at me stare at me and
now they look sideways
    at one another

and smirk

now they all
take a hit off a joint

and pat each others' fannies
as if in thanks
    for something

weird motherfuckers
          my
     demons

GAGAKU

my message for the critics?
           leave me alone

it's too late to make me
                and my
                      work famous

I've worked 24 years and
if I've discovered a single
truth it's this:

                fame
              attention
                praise
              only
          makes me
                fat
            of head

this does not mean my work should
  be rejected en toto

print the good ones the
alive ones the
      workers

gagaku

what I want does
not
exist

I know
I've looked

all over

so I'm given to live without
getting what I want

if it's to be
  make do

I will
go on doing this

there is no choice when what one
wants does
not exist

I do not want an
                award
  all I want is a civilized
                mate and it
                        does
not exist

they want things upon things
and
or
trip upon travail
or

and lots of hugging
and their breath is
                amiss
none of them want me
writing this kind of poetry
they
want
science fiction and film scripts and
                  plays

once

in a while
it's good to fill a page, hear the machine talk
rappity bam bam.   "the world is a piece of meat" I
say aloud and wonder if I should write it. I place
marlboro in ashtray and write it. junkie
neighbor coughs. I hear him waiting for me to cough
up 60. No. better to blast this poor page
than rise and go to money
hidden in small mag

only lamantia wrote honest about the opiate demon.
A 10 page thing I never never see anywhere.
Censored. By the frizzles

and frizzles hate the above.
I used to bellow how only art had no dead end
I knew
I was wise
These fellows like Pound & Bukowski & Henry Miller
& D H Lawrence and others
all of them take stances
and it's impossible to talk to them
dead or alive
gone or here
they are successful.

they would say, "leave more between lines."

demons clap and laugh, it's good I see them
and better I write.   they dance... look at me while
they dance

some have stopped dancing, and look at me
those that dance wrap arms around ones who've

stopped
and try to swing them into action

now they all wave books, some by me..most by others
now they read from books and they read while they
dance and now now

they sit and read, studious. now they peek up over
their book.   blink blink blink
                          blink

gagaku

I've read a few published
poems of late
that call poem writing a psychiatrist
a therapy

and indeed
this is the way I see poem writing too

when I get angry at other humans
when I really want to slice them

I come here to this typewriter
and somehow the anger subsides a bit

enough so I don't slice them

it could be I'd be better off if I did
slice them

their ears
genitals
arms toes
heads from the bridge of the nose up

all off
    off

Audience

today I saw BARFLY
        and the place was packed
and when the writer's name

        came on the screen in the
                beginning titles
1 young woman hissed
        and one young man
        clapped loud and
                for real

the
        rest of us
                kept quiet

gagaku

I see a tiny white thread
caught
in the hair
upon my
wrist

I remove it

now all is
ready

calm

relaxed

untenuous and
untense

I Need A Woman Here Bitching At
me

I've
Been Too
Long Without A
cunt.

A Lesson I Don't Forget

I fell in love
with her ass
—it was not only her ass that
caused me to
fall
in love with her ass but her back shoulders
        in fact all her white
           skin
     not a blemish except one
        human finesse
            by that I mean a single lovely pink
    mole behind her neck
  just behind her right shoulder blade
          no no
     collar bone?
anyway her ass I fell so much in
    love with I often
   fantasized
  about it until one day I got the
       chance and did stick my tongue up it
       and you
know—it tasted just like

    feces
      human feces
  but still
now that she's gone I
     fantasize about her
        ass—it hasn't stopped
   but no longer do I think the
    grass is greener

gagaku

undercover demons
            peek up
            over edge of satin sheets and the
            color of satin is silver or
                        lighter but not
                                    white

            mercury color
            maybe

    2 days ago at
    Honsu Massage
    Violet

did everything I wanted
                        but
                        still it took hard
                        labor from her

                    about 20 minutes of
                motion and
            ringing and
            tumbling-like
                        motions

        a real bed
        room exercise

    I had to be there because of a severe
                headache
            ringing my
                right brain

only orgasm would clear it and

only at Honshu
was it done

I couldn't do it myself
the pain was far too
great

The Threat

                         4 girls were over here
drinking with me
        and 2 decided they would stay and sex it up
                                 with me when I
unclothed myself

it started when one of the girls asked me
                  what I wanted to do

I said take off my clothes and
                  she said go ahead

I did
then two of them did too

the other two got huffy and said they
                    had to go
  and they did
            they left

the 3 of us still here had big sex
                        rita was 16
            and bernice was 19

 I was more attracted to rita
                  so much more that
            bernice angered and said
      I COULD GET YOU INTO A LOT OF TROUBLE

so I left rita for a bit and
    humped a little on bernice
                this quieted her down

gagaku

I'm getting too
precious with my
feces
too sacred with my
organ cap

too holy
with my
memory of those
cute
vaginas in my
          distant
past

now they swing before my memory again
there's one with a cute
freckle on the
left labia

there a big juicy one
yes
and there's a dry 1
looks good but
          dry

she gave absurd
head

there's an
ugly 1 but I
        fuck it anyway

there's one I went down on
but came right back up

when I got a
            whiff

reeking fucking thing—it was horrible
so I just screwed it and played
pattycake with the sensitive
                                breasts
she wanted our relationship to be more sexual so
she didn't wash it before we went out to
a topanga dinner

there's one that has fingers in its lips
knowing moving pressing squeezing

gagaku

I figure
kill'em on my page
that way I don't have to
kill'em in real
life

a simple cretin's therapy
I go licking her arms off
tongueing her eyes out
biting off that fine aquiline
          nose

ramming my skull's forehead
into those perfect
     teeth

swing my right fist
catch her in ribs
knee her where she lost her
     balls

squeeze each buttock
grab that flesh harder
pull it
off

they may of
course call me a sadist
and if I am
not in my poem
a sadist that is
my poem is a
failure

259

got her now
she's a bleeding wreck
I figure
best to kill her here

kiss tongue fuck do the best
I can to
love
her in actual life

It's a concept and concepts rot
but so far so
    good

gagaku

    it is
    not such a bad
        life beating out
        a few poems now
            & then
    Mencken wouldn't
        call this poetry
      and I like him

      merely disagree with
        him

     I like much of what he wrote
         in defense of women

   I like
   to write in
      defense of
       demons

   I actually see them
      here when I write
         with finger bells on

    and leather loin coverings

I can write of their brass
      or gold ear rings
      or the stripping
       of their loin cloths

      and waving big
        organs and bulbous
       testicles about

it makes little difference to
        me long as I write of them

    it makes little difference whether
    you or someone else
               considers it
    obscene or
        not poetry

gagaku

pinched her ass
        she smiles
pulled up her jersey blouse
        sucked her nipples
she wants to fuck
     they mirror us
but let me tell you
   I just
farted: a sign of life!
      & let me tell
        you: demons
       are staying out of sight
      back in blur
fuzzed
cowards!   chickenshits!
  come out.
let me see you.
what am I if I cannot
      describe you?
come out.
I plead with you.
demons. please. come out!
     if I cannot see you
you stay trapped within my ribs
               poison my gut
   cause my exterior fist to slam
             into another human face.
you cause it to pick up blade or firearm
        if I cannot
     see you. come out!
   I implore you.
they weave in a curved line
      like a sidewinder snake
     all of them

        holding 1 tamborine

amongst them.

they are smug

I've admitted my dependence

Judgment

                    the most beautiful woman
                    I have ever seen
                    told me I was
              arrogant
            insightful
         honest
          and self
                indulgent

and I lie here
   sticking my thumb nail
       into the filter end
            of my

         cigarette
      and I'm alone

   also she told me she was perfect
            and she was
            and she told me she
            was just folks
         and I don't know
         if she was just folks

   what are just folks?
   and she told a black waitress hot chocolate
   when asked for her order
                and I was jealous
            I thought she was
         coming on to the waitress

   and she told me I was a
      crazy man

"oh you crazy man"
   is how she said it

and once she told me
     "I like
   furry animals" as she
rubbed her fingers
     upon my chest

that was before she said
   "get out of my
       life fucker"
       and meant
         it

gagaku

the guy's wife keeps
              prodding urging
                        motivating him
I miss out on all this
I keep alone and
jerk
every several days

eyeing a penthouse mag
not fun
but
demons wave me off
my sex habits are private they tell me

keep to
new visions of
                us
they tell me
 keep describing us

now I look at my right palm for some reason
 the gagaku record has finished up

everything's
fucked

I'll go restart the music and
try to imagine demons

that's not true either
there's no trying

sometimes I'm sure it's conjury
now I see them banging cymbals together

shiny brass
and I think of Phil and his demons
in Wilmington
up on the hill
looking down at a freighet
frei   frieghter coming in - it's lights
                at night
a man either finds a way through his own disgust
 or fuck fuck fuck fuck fuck
                        fuck to the
                            fifth

never give a woman a book of poems
unless they're by sylvia plath

I can't even remember what
it's like—where is that woman?
 or
her or
    her

gagaku

                  terse
       it's
noisy & terse &
                  hurts me rather than
                       gets me to want to
                              read
                              it

  poem writing keeps monsters
                         off
                    the streets

   at least as long as they are typing
                   me
                   too

I feel worse
      than death - yet if I stub my
                  toe now
I'll

                  where was I?
                    they blink
                       play with their dick again
                    & now their breasts
                    now stick a talon in their navel
                         eye their lint
                  laugh
            vomit on their chest
                  shake it off
      great creatures I see
                    and
                    have seen

gagaku

by now if you are old enough to be reading
this you know human life can be
extraordinarily
cheap
10 friends I've lost
though admittedly I use the term friends
loose

drugs didn't kill them
drugs were just their tool
psych-weakness killed them
and I watched many moments of their falling
trying to help but in some cases
aiding their death rather than hindering
it

not consciously
consciously I sought to help
make them see something
worth more life
but no
they wouldn't see
angered at me for my
meddling

demons cluck about their caskets
I see demons walking around celebrating
at those 10 humans' caskets
all laid out in a decagon

demons raise their claws and extend their talons straight
up

and shout

I see them shouting
    and dance now grasping arms and swinging
   each other about in couples
  there are 10 or
  20 demons
  all dancing

round the caskets of my friends
    wooden pine boxes unpainted
       and unvarnished
  raw pine wood holds each of my
    pals

gagaku

definitely vulgar
    I like to
        eat hookers out
     Japanese ones

  as they eat me out
 I like very few white women that well

   as a General Rule white women take
   much worse care of their
     vaginas than Japanese

   though I've
     loved exceptions

     it seems dozens of times
       each day
   I actually (though alone) say out loud
(with someone in mind)
   fuck you

     and I
     really get angry
   for a few
   seconds

   then it passes
    totally away
  and the person I was angry
 with is kind once more in my
    psyche
just a female editor I've never met
  way back east
    who actually has published some of

me me my work

        how about john marquand?
read his "ENDGAME"

      I like to
skip around
  I'm very free here
and if you
  don't like it I
    don't like

   you

gagaku

               last night
          first woman in 10 months
               a jap hooker
               a little older
                    than most
               more relaxed the
               thing was I
               had been reading
                    robert herrick and
          he mentioned
          buying the same sort
                    of
     grub

we need our god damn grub once in a while or we go
                    plum stale

               and if it doesn't come to our
                         front door and jump on us for
               our terrific artistic
                              talent

               then we must go to the store or turn
                    plum stale

          once a year
               is enough for me

          when it's as well done as you-
               me
          does it
          yumi that is
     if you need a woman
come over here and I'll take

you to her

       if you're a woman
         you stopped reading
           this poem in the
           fourth line
     you're not even here
       when
            ...yes yes yes you
                 should be
               ashamed of
                yourself!!!

women

                        once you've
            slept with them
                for some time

                will
                finally
                get over on
            their
        hands and knees
                nude

        and you
            behind and
                    in them
                will hear
                a kind of
            deep gutteral
            snickering

        it's there—demon
            even if I
    misspelled guttural

        it's there-demon and
        I heard
    it several times from
        several women

        a deep bad kind of laugh
        like I've got your dick
        now motherfucker

I
own
you

gagaku

how deep is my violence
     deep as I can shock
                    intestines with a fist
                    right up your ass
                        grab those worms
          hold them up to
               ...
there's no need to write here
          no need to live
                    no hope
          no beauty
     all is cold and
     ...
demons hook their wrist
                    about my neck
                    pull me to them
                    kiss me on cheek
                    I smile
               they push me away
                    I see the bottoms of their shoes
                    small adlai stevenson hole
                         in sole
                         ...
          never have the streets seemed so empty
                    so sad
          I was told this would happen by
                    the best writers
          but to see such bleakness
                    and know it is not my projection
                    but
          truly the way
          it is
          ...
one flower smiles

its petals actually curl up at ends
it is happy
I don't know its make
lily or rose or pansy or marigold
or daisy
and it smiles
…
this is not enough

gagaku

    he writes the way he
                  wishes

for him
   prose is

   work

   poetry—

       l
        o
         v
          e

over

& over &
over he reads his
own poems that are
printed in the small
mags trying to figure
himself

first he goes out &
gets breakfast
driving 25 miles up
PCH to Paradise
Cove where at Sandcastle
restaurant he sups

two poached and a belgian
waffle with honey and butter and
maple syrup and coffee no juice
but yes water and
the highway patrol men who eat
        there too
behind his back put a nail in
one of his goodyear eagles
in the sidewall where it costs
200 to fix
a new tire is a must

then he drives home slower
not so fast as up PCH with
that 1990 5.0 liter fuel
injected
mustang

and he smokes a bit of drug
heroin

and when they question him upon his poetry
he claims FICTION IT IS ALL PROSE FICTION
and he reads over & over his
published poems trying to figure
himself

he's curious about himself because he
is himself he is not you as he used to
think he was when into the oneness
                              nonsense
heroin heroin heroin tar almost black mexican
tar heroin something to boost an artist in
constructive pain kill long as he's
temperate with it
moderate with it
very
careful with it

in santa monica

order "PASTA RICHMOND"
at Bono Fortuna
        Cafe
on Main Street

angel hair spinach
        pasta
with sliced olives
& mushrooms (both
free) & some tomato
        pieces
—if too many tomatoes
send it back for more
olives & mushrooms
(tell them steve
told you to)

ah so

9:38 P.M. & the
artist Ken Kishi
has just showed up

I like him—he
  taught me

ga means gorgeous
       and
gaku means music

gagaku

the older I get the more animalistic
                              humans
                                 appear

                        there are the christians
                                 the gays
                              the members of islam
                              the jews
                           the blacks
                         the poets
                              often I realize how preposterous
                                 this is

useless in
              fact harmful to
                    blank
                    paper

there are too
              many poets for
                              the
                                 trees

ants don't have to do this
                        things are better for them
              they know what they're about
                           always an
                                 object
                           a
                        goal
                     a
                  task

I don't see ants

overdosing
weeping
having staff meetings
I don't see ants having
to make a living
being bored
onth'job
at least I can walk up and down the beach a mile
a day
and sing

gagaku

          I
like short poems best

        I like early cummings
                    when he was
                        still making a
                                bit of
                                 ¢

gagaku

she's back in jail
            after only 2 weeks

when she was
            caged
                        she gained 40 pounds
                                    and looked perfect

I could tell
            in my
                        bed

but now she's back in prison
                                    I know
                                                because she called
                                                            collect

she likes crack &
                        heroin

she kicked methadone
                        legal clinic methadone
            80 milligrams a day
            (though she jawed some to
                                                sell)
                        by smoking
                                    crack

she just likes crack
            and knows how to prepare it
                        (baking soda)

gagaku

        she takes a shower
       has been here a little
               over 4 months
           it's 1991
          early 1991
      and I didn't feel
     I would share this cave again
but she has come in
     and has stood off my rantings
           & angers
             yellings
               cussings

    ravings
      and so far
        she has stayed
       and most th'time
  91
    percent of our time
it's
 fun

muse

here now
  a great woman
  I say so
     she's my
    not my woman
  THERE IS
      NO SUCH THING AS MY
             WOMAN
OR MY
   MAN

OR
my
    anything

gagaku

the girl tells me there's only 1 thing I have to do

    keep writing

"all you have to do is keep writing"
                  she tells me

the rest is unimportant
            spending money & paying bills
                driving my 2 mustang f liter
                          hot
                        rods

    f stands for
           five

maybe there are few performance car enthusiasts among
            poetry readers

    most my readers didn't inherit 50
                grand
so as to buy 2.5 liter mustang
            hot
        rods

GAGAKU

no girls here for many weeks
        this is fine
I am relaxed
    girls make me nervous and
                        guilt ridden
                    why?
because I'm too young for them
                    51
and I havn't learned yet
                    learned
                how to
        be
supportive
            warm
            reliable
and sober

no
I am more obsessed with this
                        writing wife
                    than any woman
                            on earth save
Aphrodite
and it's been 15
                years since I last
                        eyed her
those
    sparkling eyes
    that radiant skin
            that
            ABSOLUTE
beauty
    that
    perfect

voice

that
unconquerable

ALLURE

GAGAKU

somehow
    a writer has to have enough money not to
    dwell on it inside
                her or his
                    mind
  once I was close to a
truly great scribe
            and in speaking about money he said,

"not too much...not too little"

ah well
birds are right now chirping a bit as they feed on the
                wildbird seed
  gagaku music plays right now
        soothing me some

      it's hawaiian like weather outside
             lovely storm clouds
                  clear blue between thunderheads
     I last saw Aphrodite in person
            15 years ago

      we met by mistake or
   fates

    I touched her left shoulder
      the problem was that I could not share her
      and aphrodite is above all
            in need of more than one
                fellow

once she said, "I don't want to play cat and mouse.."

then I found out she was born in 1948
year of the rat

a libra
a libra rat goddess
once I was close to a truly great scribe
and in speaking about woman he said,

"sometimes 1 night is
enough"

gagaku

God?   preoccupied with th'idea
                    feeling
                         of God?
Nietzsche?
        Bukowski?

always scribbling of
                God? His
not being real
the excuse of believing in Him
                    as a disease
all
that

not I

it's demons for me
a case of simple exorcism
getting them out of my belly
                my ear
                lobe
                        my
rectum
    hair

getting them th'fuck
            out
        here in my
                work

they can
call it art
        they can call it work
they can call it lame

               they can label it
                       silly
                       shit

my demons
               agree
nod their face at me

gagaku

not having written poems for months
I'm full of them now
and they roll out of me
like. . .
anything you want to imagine

it's what I do best and
what I do easiest
but it isn't going to make me
famous
like a best seller
novel
and I want that
I'm not perfect
I want that

maybe I just
think I want it
usually I get what I want
I nag the world
until it comes

so why not a novel?
why not 'best seller' fame?
it's no fun
for me
it starts as fun to write
such a thing
then it stales after 30
40 pages

fuck it
I'll stick here
 in the

short devastating poem
the demon poem
the mad poem
the sick poem

where I'm
comfortable

gagaku

　　　　if I'm lucky I'll
　　　　　　　　be
　　　　　　86 toking a joint and writing
　　　　　　　　　　a
　　　　　　　　　poem
　　　　not
　　　　　　prose

　　　I'm no good at
　prose

unless I'm on
　　　　　　heroin
　　　　　　to cut the back
　　　　　　　　pain

　　　and since I
　　　　　　do
　　　　not snort nor
　　　　　　smoke heroin anymore because

it's
silly

I'll be smoking a
　　　joint if I'm 86 &
　　　　　　　lucky
and typing
right here

GAGAKI

20
or so years back I
thought I had it all
figured

why humans are
messed
up

it was mere
self hate

that's
all

now I think it's demons
humans full of demons
& humans have to exorcise their
own demons
in their own
art
work

like many I
project my reality upon
others

maybe we are packed with angels
instead

like my late
dad

he was and still
in my psyche

                        is
                an
                angel

   an innocent
too easily hurt by grasping
                                greedy
                relatives
            such
                as myself

guilt? am I full of guilt rather than demons or
                angels or demons &
                                        angels?
why
not

gagaku

freedom
where the
fuck is it?

and what is it?
a enuck?
or
how about enuch?
that looks better

my root canal hurts
just slight enough to mention

I can't get over paying
500 for an hour's work

my job is to keep an eye on 13
million of real estate

not write poems
I kid myself when I write

my job
is to write poems

this
isn't a job

this is like an affair
that won't end

the bitch is this typewriter
I love and love her and lover

what's wrong—
it is supposed to read

I love her and love her and love her
everyday about 3 or 4 times now

4 or 5 poems a time
I am this typewriter's only lover

but her name is masculine
Remington

a single name
so I'm a fag for my typewriter

spiritual homo
I've never had a cock in my mouth

save in my dreams
and it's always been mine

GAGAKU

he who says he is a sensitive fellow is NOT
same for she

he who gives you a free dime lump of crack
                    is like a SUCTION CUP WORM
                                        a suck on
                your
                soul
            and wallet
he who acts like your friend yet sexes your gal
    will come around again to see if you have
                    LEARNED

I keep from humans now
    at least here in this
            cave

    I go to cafes 2 or 3 times a day
                    and get along quite well with
                    cafe folks

        it takes th'waitresses 2 or 3 of my visits to
    realize I am not short term hustling'em

    then they begin mentioning my name among themselves
    until the famous owner himself comes up to me
with a hand thrust out for shake...he is curious of
this fellow who has his girls mentioning his name

    enough
        it's time
        my demons
            agree
                quietly...softly

nod with me

adjust their conservative tie
feel for their wallet
it's there

feel for their 2 pair of glasses
clear & dark
prescription lenses

now go to work
they're off
while I stay behind typing this
content driven off to
trabajo mucho trabajo
he or she who tell you he or she is a sensitive fellow
or woman
is not

GAGAKU

1st one this 2-16-93 morn
might be th'17th instead
around 9
AM
good old
gagaku music on
though a bit loud

now it's okay
just turned it down
gets too screechy for me when
too loud

a woman here last
night

I right now just screaming at full volume at
pal who knocks when he hears me working
typer
he thinks all this phoney
my mediocre fucking
sham art
—he thinks THEN
LIKE NOW
IT'S TIME TO KNOCK & INTERRUPT TH'LUCKY
prick

307

INTERESTING

to follow their advice
        live their advice
        practice what they
                preach

  baudelaire
      bukowski
          artaud
            rimbaud

some
    henry miller
  a speck of
who?   you?

        demons..
  I say th'word hoping they
             provide
      image

        eating
       banana
     slopping it in
        their
      messy
        maw

GAGAKU

demons?   more?

it's march 28 or 29
            '93

    are demons still
                        inside?

    maybe
rowing
    t h' d a n u b e

    It's th'only clean river in europe
                    jaques tells me tonight on
            channel 9

    hell
I'm even taping th'documentary
                    right now

demons?
                rolling gurneys along hospital corridor
                        white dresses
                                white mens' clothing
                        white sheet on me
                                    a patient
                            for some black melanoma
                                behind th'right
                                                ear
            now they're all screaming
                        at me

GAGAKU

april 29
1993
no poems typed
written
for 2 weeks
I am full of murder
I want to stick my word sward
sword
in certain living persons
I awake each morning detesting
them
2 of them
but
you know
we can't go actually murdering
living beings
without grave
truth or
consequences

GAGAKU

a chuckle
he chuckled just a bit aloud
as he wrote his gagaku

way in th'past
at least 50
seconds back

then he lit a skinny joint
still has th'smoke in his lungs
just exhaled

no chuckle now
just a steady turtle or tortoise's plodding
on

GAGAKU

may 6
        1993
around 10 AM
a bit overcast on this
            Santa Monica beach

      not a breeze in sight
        a few birds chirping

      a few cars driving up holocaust avenue

3 fat chested goldfish
           happy and busy 5 feet to my left in 20
                  gallon
              florescent lit
                tank

    gagaku music playing
some aging weird looking fellow with a
           lipoma on left shoulder
      typing
        his demons gesticulate over his right shoulder
        kibitzing to him about th'ode he's working
    he doesn't hear them yet he knows they are
  almost obnoxiously yapping away their advice

          they are so busy and happy and satisfied
      with his
    literary
    pointing
    them out

NO CRACK HERE

no woman &
no drug

thundering classic music on now
dark grey outside with
thundering rain

whoops
forgot to put wild birdseed out
about 830 AM

rain or no rain they tweet for
breakfast

please
for a minute
excuse me

now seed out
on shelf
doves and sparrows
perhaps finches
I can't tell sparrows from finches or
maybe some other genus..
doves and tiny birds wait for
breakfast

sing for me every morn

GAGAKU

2 weeks ago
around 4-23-93
I sent about 100 odes to
a fellow who requested
submission
then I apologized in a letter about
4-27-93
for sending too many

"better I'd selected
5 of the best"

is how I put
it

yesterday
or perhaps th'day
before

I received th'stack back
less 7

he had accepted 7

and so I thought
to myself
glad I sent the fat stack
glad I sent "too many"

if I'd submitted 5
how could he accept
7?

1 MAN IS HOOKED

on crack
writes ode after ode while smoking
crack
& grass

what do I
think of him?
a fool
does it really matter?
th'ode he types
his
decision about a speeding ticket?

he was going to fight it
he drove like a maniac and they sent
a no light on th'top cop
car
and he
missed it in his rear view
every 13 seconds peeking for lights
on top

for 3 years he drove like a
lunatic

oh my God it was
fun

he told me
now
he's confused

now he'll go to traffic school
now he'll

take it easy
     maybe stop in time for a
          6 year old boy
          chased across avenue by
                    eleven year old
                    brother

GAGAKU

no problem
    they'll understand
        first he was addicted to
            beer
          cigarettes
              then grass then H then
           angel dust then coca
         then off coca because it seemed
                when snorted
                    like insect poison
              then H
          then methadone
                and off H then

    crack
then crack
        CRACK YOU
      over th'psyche it does
    when you quit 1 night you
          dream of it and awake 2
        hours later & call
              beeper
        people

this is what he tells me
    I can't help
    I'm addicted myself
    to th'drug of authentic
            publication
    th'verification of
        mediocre
        soul

    I know because Aphrodite said
            so

317

demons are confused
                         as if they've lost direction
                                       bearings
               look that way & this way &
                                then
                  over there &
                                          here

ah oh— it was an act
                        contemplating their hairy.. fuzzy
                                  navel
                  and looking up then
              stabbing their own 7 inch sharp
                pointed..   middle & index talons at
                              once as if 2
        fingers in lover's
           orifice

GAGAKU

fellow named artaud
     should have been happier
              he was so wise as to write
       that
   van gogh would have been better advised by
          doctor gachet
      to go lie down and rest
  rather than
  go out in fields and paint

that day he shot
  himself in his
     tummy

           VINCENT WAS AGITATED IN
         HIS INFORMAL THERAPY SESSION THAT
               day

needed rest
just lie down and close eyes
no
need even to sleep
JUST REST
DO NOT WORK
A MAN WHO WORKS HARD IS OFTEN WORKED TO
                       DEATH
    and vincent was worked
       by his shrink
         to
       death

GAGAKU

this antique remington typer
  had many keys stick
and a horrible noise
  as I moved carriage from
left to right

I tried every yellow page typer service person
  but none wanted my old remington to work

                                     upon

probably unavailable
         parts

     so
I decided I would try to service this
  lovable machine myself

took a small oil can and
  drowned it all
         all in oil

now no keys stick
     now that carriage noise is gone
now oil gets over my paper as I type but this
  is slowly ceasing too

maybe I will start a new
  business
servicing typers over
  50 years old

my demons now give me body language message
just keep writing poems on us
     they tell me
  that is all I have to

                              do
                        t hey
          communicate

    forget about letters that skip
                              they say
              readers will understand your odes
                                    regardless
                        they
            let me
              know

GAGAKU

th'gods
including bukowski
and malob …
gave me good advice

keep writing
stay alive

they told me
even one of the goddesses told me all I
have to do is keep
writing

another:
Aphrodite
told me "it's moving…"
referring to my
scribbles

about my tree candle making she said, "they're beautiful"
then ungod ferlinghetti said about my work
"…it's interesting."
but
then said
to me, "I can see why bukowski is
attracted to your work-tell
him I'm attracted to
his"
& I did
& now city lights has made tens of
thousands of bukowski
tomes
and more than that of
dollars

it's my fault
   I wrote that cruel line about ungod ferlinghetti
                 in a satire entitled charlene
                                     rubinski

john martin of black
             sparrow offered to publish a book of
                         MY
                         WORK

     instead of saying "yes" I
                     threw a can of
                     beer against his
                     wall

something is wrong with me - I
have a personality
             defect - my demons
                    NOD

gagaku

when I've lost almost everything else
I can still win here
which is why
I'm here

now others will think me a hypocrite
because I never seem to lose
my beachside cottage
and sufficient money in my wallet

others say "you've never starved
            you don't drink enough
          you're gone
        you can't duke it
      you ripped me
    you're stingy
  and selfish
  and self centered"

yes
others say these things

so I have as little to do with
them as possible

I try to get along
maintain friendships
but it seems
impossible

so?
so I come back here
here I feel good

now alone in my place I feel good
    because I'm writing

GAGAKU

when things get really bad in the
immediate proximity
of here
RIGHT
HERE
I fight back with my strongest
weapon

this typer music
and
it
always
silences th'
enemy

GAGAKU

I liked sinatra's THE BEST
              REVENGE IS LIVING WELL

     or
LIVING WELL IS TH'BEST REVENGE

so I live well
   and all th'poets, etc
            seem to resent it
                    resent me
                       my lovely
                    garden
                       my
               wonderful
                    cave
                 on th'
                    sea

even
bukowski

GAGAKU

over 49 billion
that's how many

odes have been written on
earth
how do I know this?

a
good
question

why do I speak to
me?
because everyone else
makes me nervous
later or
sooner
or
antsy

does this mean I am
schizoid?
the old doctor thought so at my draft
physical in
1966

"I don't think you and the service would get along
together."

is the way he put
it
after classifying me 1Y

and writing "Schizoid"

on some form

maybe it's because I told him he was dead as the desk
        he sat behind and I would
                        not get on his conveyor belt
                to
            vietnam

GAGAKU

around 11AM
      sunny outside
            gagaku music on semi-quiet
          4-4-94
lots of fours
  once I published stance magazine issue #5
           after issue #3
         because I read somewhere 4
           is th'Tao
             and/or Buddhist number for
             death
     & I didn't wish to
         mess around with
           death
    though
th'first time I met Mr. Bukowski
was a night at his place on
            DeLongpre Ave
           in East Hollywood — he'd
(1965)   invited me and I'd
         walked in his place and
     been instantly stunned by his
         face—he was 44 and I
            24

            his face was
           beautiful in th'exact
        antithesis to th'"pretty"
     billboard faces and
   his face
shone all th'in toto SOUL
     missing from th'billboards faces and
after an hour of beer drinking and
    some talk he

drove me to th'liquor store and he purchased 3
       more 6 packs and
     on returning he
    opened 2 more
       and gave me one and he sat in his old
          stuffed easy chair and looked at me a
        moment
and then he said, "LET'S DRINK TO DEATH!"
    and I hesitated exactly 1 1/2 seconds and
   decided THIS MAN IS AND WILL ALWAYS BE
EARTH'S FINEST SCRIBE AND IT IS AN EXQUISITE
HONOR TO BE IN HIS CAVE WITH JUST HIM AND I &
  IF HE WISHES TO TOAST DEATH WITH ME I AM
IMMENSELY HONORED and we clanged our beer
          cans together and drank to
      d e a t h

jackie o

   died last
     night

lymphatic cancer
spread so
     fast

she was a LEO
   a material
        girl

with
so much
   style?

hey man
   I would have bedded her
              given a wee
            chance
         and even though I
       know by experience th'LEO
             girl
       doesn't care much for
                sex
       just th'stuff.. all th'stuff
               surrounding
               sex

Jackie O swore never again to
          mate with a
          handsome man
          because she said she could
never again trust an
   attractive

        man

you
 know
what I
 mean

GAGAKU

Phil smokes crack and then writes
                and sometimes his work is
                                published
            in th'noble small
                                press

        he tells me
                just a few hits
                        not too much

                    is
                his
            way

and a little grass
                maybe 2 puffs
                        or deep inhales

        he says demons sometimes appear
                in his
                vision
                and when he says
                            'vision'
                    it seems a bit
                    touched

"of course this is all I lie"
                he says
            and he scratches his head
                he seems confused
            talking as he types

he can have his demons

he says
as he
types

GAGAKU

                    this is th'way I
                         fool myself & so
                              far I
                              succeed
          I can tell each new
                         morn
                    when I awaken and
                    no
               one
               is here to
          insult
          nor criticize
                    nor false
                         flatter me

save
 myself

and I do enough for
          a whole flock of
                         us
                    so called human beings
     demons calm
          and agree
               ing with me

                    for they know too
                         how to remain
                              civil

in times of
     tenuous rationalization
                    for plain
               surviving another
                         day

336

                another
                        single
        d a y

now they wipe a tear away from their
                                        eye
                        some weep one tear from left eye and
                others wipe th'tear from their
                        other
                        eye

        "it doesn't matter" I just softly said aloud to
                                myself
        whether or not it's a true tear
                or a croc
                        odile
                        tear

GAGAKU

                    THAT HAS A SHITTY POEM
               th'one I just typed

          I want more
      kill another gal with a sizzors
                    is what I need
               on paper
               so it won't be
               on court
                    tv
I need a left claw margin
I need th'third person
he needs to
describe them throwing cantalopes at each other
               making monster faces at him
                         stretching lips
               which pull apart like large elastic bands

      "I'm babysitting myself" he repeats three times
               but keeps typing
        that's what poetry is
                    -babysitting one's self

          is what he thinks
          and thinks he knows

        so I look to my left
                         at 7 growing discus
                              fish
      now that's subtlety
      beauty is hypnotic
        it can't be conquered
          "it's like radium"

he tells himself barely
aloud

GAGAKU

        much of his money goes to
            poor drug dealers with
       kids to
    feed

many
  of his demons hand over
       money
    green currency
      to
    some vague being
         I can't make out for it's blurred

    DEMONS WAG
      A FINGER
      talon at me as if shame
          on me
       for something

  it's harmless so
     far

I got a way
    to get mine out
    most
    folks
  don't

most folks feel
    they'd be fired
      or ridiculed
      or
   lose a wife or
    husband

if they wrote on
                their demons

I think..
        maybe not
    demons?   I don't like th'word
            they don't either

it's now 4-8-94
                around midnight
                        maybe it's th'9th by now..

had some
    surprise visitor
made me anxious
        unexpected visitors make me anxious
        especially when I
                    let them
                        in

this

        takes everything
      and
maybe I should have
  done it
    some other way
        but
        but
    I feel better owing money
              than
      saving it
  better
     smoking candy
              than
      eating
    it and I feel
    this is worth
      it all
    worth
  what seems no true
        sacrifice at all but
              but
          a
        gift
     "one has to fool oneself here"
   just said aloud
   "one has to fool
       oneself here"

After

2 years on methadone
I've been off a week

Contac
cold medicine
stopped my head from
squirting
through nose and
sneeze
and spit

Excedrin PM allowed me to
sleep
at least
last night

a few puffs of
cannabis
got me to my type

I feel wonderful

gagaku

they swing along the street now
    really up on the sidewalk

    arm in arm
a woman demon with her
   man demon

 a content happy couple
  I see them walking
  along wearing sweaters

  now they stop hug
 and kiss each other
on lips now stick long
 curling & uncurling
tongues in each other's
    ears

  now I can't quite tell
what they're doing
   I see them but they're in
a bit of fog
 they're blurred
to my eye

 that's alright
I enjoy couples in love and
 they definitely are in love
 even though
they're slapping each
other now

 now each swigs a beer
from a can

long chug a lug
they seem to be competing
 seeing who can finish the
can first

 now they
 kiss really a make-up
 peck and
now they stroll
     arm in arm
       again

I

spend myc of
 my day reading
        my poems in
          the little
        mags that
        have been good enough to
publish
           them

               now I just looked up
           at the first stanza and noted
             myc

      it was supposed to be much
my body does not always do what my
                          mind
    tells it to do

    I sit here silent for about 4 minutes
   tying to figure this problem
    I come to no solution
       then type
       this last stanza

Just Smoked "Good" Grass

and just moved this typewriter by
    unintentional action
3 inches to right so that it hit an
    aluminum ashtray
I made 31 years ago in metal shop
and the result was an oriental type
bong noise
very musical
wish it was longer
can't have everything
never complete sastisfaction forever
we humans bitch and bitch and bitch
    and bitch
or should I write complain instead?

I know I do
I bitch and bitch and bitch

not to other humans mostly
mostly to myself
I am always complaining to myself
well
not always

for instance
not now

now I'm working
way off in the distance I hear a dog
    barking
very muffled
I can barely hear it

the subject for a poem?

just walk around the block
said Bukowski

please, please

I want to write a bad poem
1 that truly doesn't work
what's important is that to my own
eye it flops utterly
  that's hard
I please so many others
writing what their eye
says flop failure not even poetry

but not to my own eye
it likes my work too much
it will simply
 love
this poem

that's not what I want
it would be so easy to
        fuck this poem up
fuck fuck shit shit feces feces
            anal anal stick it stick it

cock a suck a doodle doodle
there
I'm feeling
better
        already

GA GA KU

why not?
it should be GAGAKU
but this typer skipped

typer? is that a Buk word? a Pound word?
who wrote TYPER
                first?
does it
matter?
demons wave their face side t o
                s i d e

I guess they don't
            think
                so

it is shorter than TYPEWRITER
demons now revolve their face in oval
                        round and round like an egg
                            from
                    my eye right in front of
                            them
now?
a pall
a personal worry
        a going down that
                    refuses
                        to
                deaccelerate

demons laugh
        smoke a big cigar
    they knew it all th'
                time

350

GAGAKU

the editors are furthering their own writing careers
with 2
exceptions
marvin malone
al berlinski

and I have sent both far too many poems
so th'thousands of odes I write are
in truth
quite unwanted

by all
ALL
th' others

there may be several more exceptions
but I truly doubt
it

GAGAKU

maybe you better stop writing about demons
and stop writing to gagaku music

a former pal
told me about 17
years ago

h e
quit writing himself
or at least quit submitting to magazines where I
might read his own
work

h e
I'm told became th'head of a local
teachers' union and
presides over giant assemblies of
pedagogues

h e
is a Leo and
sun folks need to
          preside over
meetings of small groups at roundtables and
big groups at assemblies and readings and
just groups of other
folks

sun folks need to
sit with groups and
shit th'shoot

I am th'opposite
then

again on occasion I find my own informal
group

maybe sitting at a bar a block away at yucatan
cafe with 3 other
folks and shitting th'
shoot

ah
it's good to write a so called poem
without any so called evil
spirits

GAGAKU

                submitting poems
                          just
                enveloped up about 30 new
                          odes &
                addressed them to
                                wormwood
                        enclosed SASE

          I like to send a poem like th'above because
              it just seems right
                          when th'last 2 words of th'last
                                        2 lines
                                  end in th'same
                                          space

        however
            I've been known to contrive: move the
                                  carriage
                          back or forward a
                              space or 2
                        to
                  accomplish all this..

demons wince
          stick tongue out
                    a pointed
              thing colored just like a
                      healthy human
                          thing

        thing...
      not much of a
                word

                            354

wormwood
    now that's
    something.

GAGAKU

7-31-93 or maybe it's 8-1
and mary
mary came over last night
or maybe just before dark

she'd been at sybil brand's place for 3
                                    months

went in weighing 80 pounds and came out 135

that white skin of
                hers
        gives off good light
                actually better than mere
                                    good

so refined and alive and
                just goddamn
                    perfect

and her face
            now so full and
    at 43
            so pretty and warm and lethal and lovely and
                not
a single female had been in this shack for
            3 months and
        I figured best not to touch mary
        because I don't want to be th'BUTCHER

in jail they fatten them up and release them over & over to be
    sliced to pieces again and again by
                BUTCHERS

8
     mabye 9 times they have fattened mary from 80 to 135
     yes
     they save her life over & over because they
   bust her only when they believe she will die
                              within days if they don't
all th'cops in venice and santa monica
             and probably culver city know
                              her

she reminds them of their
      daughter

gagaku

my life
is quite lonely
        but I endure it
                    even want it
                        this way

no woman exists to make it better
                        because I scoured our
beachball—its surface
                I looked &
                        studied all the women on
                                earth
        and
the one that came
        closest
        just told me I was a crazy
                            man
and
she wanted to be
                rich
                    anyway
        which I could understand—because as a kid
                                    she
                        suffered from a lack
of funds

she married a bass violist
one of those tuxEdoed men
a supporter of classical music

I'm a jack off poet—what would she want with me?
just
so I wouldn't be lonely? not

enough
for
her

GAGAKU

smoke too much?
 tobacco?
  crack?

cut down
 easy to say
 and crack is so ill
                tasting at times
                not so hard to do

 I lie
plato was right
 I am a liar

the poets
are all lairs

he said
I know I should speak for myself
              that
          somewhere there is a poet
                      who doesn't
                          fib

my demons?
signalling me now
            that
            they
            are not mine
             at all

        that they belong only
                  to themselves

that
they're self
    possessed

gagaku

I took henry miller at his word
                the artist should not marry
                        so I haven't

        sex   '
            is around and available for
                any artist worth
                                his
                            pepper

he will reject it more than
                    accept it

demons are
        now
        flushing some white tile toilet and
                    the water is bluish

            must have an aroma pellet

    demons
        now juggle
                still inside the tiny bathroom
                            fruit
                    they juggle yellow
                        delicious apples
                    green
                        pears
                    yellow
                        long
                    14 inch
                            bananas

                    regular oranges

                   now they
           juggle yellow and green and white
                tennis balls
            orange too

  8
     or 9
       of them

gagaku

someday I won't see my demons anymore and
thus
won't write of them
anymore

period
damn
I want to do it forever

I want that
demon

bad word—immortality

in actuality
I want to write of them forever and do
what I do forever
between my
poem writing

good meals on
main street

nope
they shake their face nope at me

I will die too
in a second
or
　　more

I don't like this
fucking idea of
　　　dying

me or anyone else
      I don't
         enjoy
           it

the demons give me a croc tear
expression—facial
they
don't give a fuck that I don't
want to ever die

gagaku

he smokes too much
    there is no hope for him
      no matter how good
         or bad
    he is with words
  written
   words

years back
    when he was
       pliable
  malleable

    he saw a page in an evergreen
             review
   with 4
    photos of artaud

it changed him forever
    he became an excessive smoker
he cussed in his poetry
  he began
     all drugs
   he wanted to go where artaud had
        gone
        &
       beyond
  he wanted to get there first and
        write about
        it

maybe if he'd never seen those photos of artaud
he would be a lawyer now

the world is full of death and maybes
the world is full too of beautiful young women
more every year—as I get older they get prettier and
firmer and more desirable—I wish I knew how to
make love to all of them at
                              once

this ode is all messed up and I know it
gener I mean gender is wrong, everything's wrong—demons
                                        themselves

seem to order me with a stern motherly look
to crumple this very sheet
and eat it—I
              will not—a man who takes orders from
his demons is

gond I mean gone

BONO

fortuno
cafe
better than my cave with all my fucking privacy
there're people in here
lovers softly laughing over espresso
they just got up & left
when I pulled out my marlboro pack

I'm a little shakey
this is my first ode written anywhere outside
my cave for 22 years

but it is silent—no typer clakking—cheap
ballpoint—there're girls in here but I eye
this sheet

who would want to dream up demons now? in
this cafe? pretty girls behind the bar—I
sit alone now at bar writing—printing in fact
I should yell out loud
a woman sings jazz-blues over sound system
she sings of love—she's singing to her lover

oh the coffee tastes wonderful
I'm still shakey—this for me is experiment
it has been lonely writing thousands alone in
my cave—a guy just
came in asking.

"excuse me excuse me could you tell me where
the OAR HOUSE is?"

gagaku

I open wormwood 108
read Buk's two poems
one about speed
one about the usefulness
of a shrink

no doubt

2 great poems
the word great is
just
almost right they are great

demons suck
each other off
a group of them
        all with dicks and
                somehow
            cunts too

the girl-waitress down at my
                favorite cafe told me
        an hour ago she read stance 5 and
found the poems a bit
                dirty
            real and making sense

she's from denmark and I wanted her to get a
dessert of
modern american
        filet

heroin

is a better reference point
than say a bad war
say Vietnam

or lebanon or
anything but a battle against adolf
but this is about heroin
    another sort of war
percodans and codeines and
                        morphine and
all the opiates
including heroin

now I scratch my forehead wondering where to
go from my reference point
        H

I would say
my meth clinic has saved my ass though
                    they really
                only wanted my
                        145 a
                            month

they have a sign on their wall—the wall
of the dosing room
where the nurses prepare my
                    saving grace

it says COWS MAY COME
            AND COWS
                MAY GO

as long as their cows keep paying their

                    mother
                    fucking

fees
they'll
save my poem-making
                    udders

gagaku

so many relationships have gone
begun endured for a bit and ended
to the continuing sound of myself
typing

my sounds
must reach a dozen apartments

I suppose some frustrated scribblers have moved

some of those with writer's block

they couldn't understand how I continued
decade after decade

folks are always
trying to
prove how I am
not living
and they
            are

and they prove the opposite
their effort
proves they are
                    miserable and hopeless

perhaps I want to think this is so and this is
not so

I remember reading a few months ago from Dos
and he was explaining how they attempt to
make the writer doubt himself
doubt his own dues paid for genius

their most potent weapon is an opaque ignoring

they do this best
they don't have to make insipid excuses
they don't have to write anything

I still make mistakes
2 days bac k
I interrupted my methadone counselor
I should have let her be—I had a urine test to take and
I was waiting for the juice to flow so I thought I'd
see the woman—I shouldn't have done it—
I should have
waited for her to tag me at the dose desk

gagaku

you take the editor who
hacked my poems in half
then printed in a random
house antho

he was a correspondent of miller henry
he was
always trying to be famous on
henry's talent

it didn't work
just like my poem
chopped at waist
did
not work

random or not

gagaku

     poetry?
      important?
      in a world like this?

only to the
        maker

and later
maybe to somebody with a problem
                        that
                the poem will
                 come nearer to
                       solving

GAGAKU

during the LA riots
I too
thought it useful
if I had a gun
but I did not have a gun
for I always figured I might use it on
me
in a fit of
depression

and as soon as the national guard showed I
knew it was over

now my demons have a shotgun and uzi and
a k 47
and
a big double shotgun
in addition to that first
smaller 1

and they shoot each other
and laugh and shoot themselves in
foot in knee in
hoof and
they shoot their own
gnarled talons right
off and they
laugh and none of them
fall
now they all
bleed a bright shiny
yellow
blood
a ferrari yellow

gagaku

yes
  when I stop I
       die

there's nothing else to my
                life
               but
          my incessant
                   creation

     Of
   My
  Own
Inside
   Me
   Monsters

3.

th'poem
knows
when
it's
over

gagaku

3-2-07
about 9 p.m.

hearing gagaku music
                now

1st time in 5 to 10
                years

demons peeking
and
waving
            my way

their fingers (talons?)
together

                    now they
            slow motion
shake their faces side to
                    side

"do they want me to stop?" I hear
            myself ask
                    aloud

gagaku

time to create
          again
     after
          10 or so
               years of
                    nada

create my demons
get'em
     out of me

gagaku

fuck a
    typer

write with a
    BALL POINT

it's quieter
            THRU
        these paper
            thin
        crack motel
                walls

gagaku

she knocks
    I open
she asks to borrow
            ten dollars

she is
    Aphrodite
I say "I
    am sorry"

she will flush
       it
     down th'crack
toilet

she says she needs it for
         rent
  but she always
  always
       fibs

  she is
  Aphrodite

gagaku

I'm 66 1/2 and writing
    again

        "that's
          awesome,"
Aphrodite
   tells me.

what a lucky man
    am I
  to have her
    as
  my muse.

sure she steal my wits
   at times—
has me undress
    then
  changes her
     mind

but if I have to be a
   fool

  it's usually worth
    it

gagaku

no poems for last 10 years
now I write poems again

something to do again
th'girls wanted me to write
                    once more

but this is for
                    me
      not
      them

they really don't care
they've their own obvious
            problems

only I
        care

just me
        and
    my sensitive
          demons

gagaku

when writing longhand be
                    sure
to
write   (or print)
    very
    carefully

this
    I
learned
    in ABNORMAL
        PSYCHOLOGY

at
U.C.L.A

demons giggle
I
amuse
my own
        demons

        they laugh their asses
                    off

their butts
fall to th'ugly
            cement

gagaku

what's the'damn hurry?
    I'm
  not going
        anywhere
I
        have
        not already been.

    I
have some
    gruesome
        unspeakable
            memories

"nothing illegal" I whisper to
                        me

sometimes a man
    falls in love
      with a woman's
        anus

it can go on for then
        maybe fifteen
           years

"until another beautiful
    asshole
        comes along," I hear

gagaku

people creep from
    room
     to room to room to
         room

a crack
  motel

gagaku

eh TV
    is
     ugly
all of it
all those
false expensive
        boiling

teeth

demons?
    Aphrodite called
        me
      this morning

then called
   back
  five more times
     for
  five different
    men

that's just how she is
     take
    her or leave
      her

gagaku

sometimes
     a man
        needs
          to
   defend
        himself against
Aphrodite,
            his
          own demons,
              and
          inflation

gagaku

Swedenborg
   can
  have
    th'angels

Dante
  th'demons

    I'll grab a decent
       breakfast
     when possible

gagaku

"little knick-knacks
                of
             shit"
say I

            pondering
                 my
             last glib
                     ode

this is 2007
         they say

      time based on a
              probably fictional
                     Jesus

demons demons
                  demons
         I don't
         know about
              golems

      demons know about
                  everything

      I can tell.

gagaku

bickering continues
        here
   among motel
      residents this
     6:30
     A.M.

crazy dopers
    worse
    than peace loving
      demons

gagaku

"hobbies save our lives"
                said
            or wrote
        Balzac

demons?
    I don't know

angels? ask
        Swedenborg

    me?
    all I do
        is
    sneeze
        twice

"I like sneezing" I
                murmur
    "it's my hobby"

 8 or 10 sneezes each
                day
    usually in
            pairs

gagaku

Aphrodite here almost all day
      very sad——
I can't make either of us happy

demons point a very sharp talon
in a slow pan
      almost a semi circle
they move that talon tip
            in a
         horizontal arc

I don't know what it means
   BUT
  it takes me somewhat
            away
      from
      this failed
            day

gagaku

OH WELL
      FUCK
how I fucked up
  how I couldn't find
    what space
            if
       any space
          I
     was supposed to
               fill
I can't relate
  to a genuine
        beautiful
        female

I am out of time
     occupying
wrong space

        OH
     poor piddling
      asshole
      me

NOTHING helps
ART
    doesn't

so? JUST FUCKING WALK AROUND
until I FALL and can't get up.

gagaku

Aphrodite is a
      courtesan
   "rather a whore" say I
     aloud to
      myself

she is always th'sexiest
woman
     around

she grabs a man's
       libido
        for her own

pisses in his toilet
       before his
     discriminating eyes

as she leaves she says "if I
never see you again…"

"I'll always remember you,"
        he
      says
and again for the
       umpteenth
        time

they
    kiss
  goodbye.

gagaku

too precious th'way
         my
    demons dance

        too slow
        motion precious

like I walk th'streets
        these days   (2007)

I think I'm hot demon
                    shit

 I have a FAT
        DEMON
            HEAD

MY HUMILITY ABOVE
            is
        complete
            BULLSHIT.

my demons? they hide

gagaku

this still saves me
    ——66 years old
            almost 66 1/2
    and this hearing gagaku
    music
    & writing to
            it

saves my sorry
            rear
    at least
    for these minutes

        these present
            units
            of time

demons laugh
        as if they don't
        believe
            me

gagaku

my demons dance
        like
     Van Gogh's
            prisoners
taking
       their
     circular
          walk

black robed
    gray robed
       too

gagaku

enough for tonight

    8 poems are
        enough

    demons nod

    file out of this
      concert
      hall

    (my one
      room
    flop)

gagaku

Aphrodite was here
        today
    WORKING
        me
without much
        success

she shows me her
        BODY
        as she changes
        clothes
        again &
            again

I say
    "YOU'RE DANGEROUS"
and she
        laughs

    she's (as they say)
        TH'
    BOMB

gagaku

Aphrodite
    comes &
        goes

   don't chase
     her

   you'll only
    walk
     into a
       breadslicer

    let
     her
       come
    &
      let her
go

gagaku

writing poems
     no
  one will likely
     read

demons weep a false
           tear
     for
     me

they don't care
     &
   why should they?

    now
  they jump up &
         down
    like
  spoiled ass
      holes

gagaku

same derelicks
    around

I'm
  one

scribbling this useful
                nonsense

useful?
demons give a
            slow
              stupid
            nod

both kinds—narcotic
          &
          YES

404

gagaku

I write these
   as if
 they'll endure

      a kind of hoax
        upon
           myself

Aphrodite once told me
    "nothing lasts."

I was trying
   to
 make her &
      I
    last

"don't
   try," she
      advised.

gagaku

all
angel wants is
      money
        for
           crack

 demons
       disagree
"they seem to know
             more than
                I"

      say I aloud now
           to
           me

now they talk mock-
            serious
     to
     one
    another

gagaku

I want
    ARTAUD
I miss
    ANTONIN

havn't read him
        for
        years

why didn't they
    give
            him heroin
when
    he begged?

what
  harm to give ARTAUD—
            one
        of Earth's
        greatest writers

    some
    simple
        effective
        junk?

POWER HUNGRY BASTARDS
SUPRA-MONSTERS CALLED
        DOCTORS

gagaku

crackheads pounding
        on
     motel doors
         for
           their
momentary
    escape

idiots
   and on occasion
          I
     join'em

gagaku

Jesus
 there are
  some
   attractive
    females
     here
      at this crack
            motel.

one just walked
        by
  I often keep th'
     front
   door
   open to
      see'em
     & get fresh
           air

 there's no back
        door

lucky th'waterbugs keep
                to
     other
  rooms so far

gagaku

getting laid
        reasonably right
                used
                    to
temporarily solve
                    frustration

        some
            coarse bitch is
                    singing
        out
    in th'courtyard

            she's so
                    happy
        she's
        sad

demons ignore all th'above
        they
            want 100% of
                    my
        poetic
                attention

            now
        they're happy

    clap claws
        clap inner ankle
                    bones
                    too

410

gagaku

leave people
            alone
        they all
            each & every
                    one
are suffering
        way
            way too much
                    to
            bad
            mouth'em
                in
                person

        Balzac taught
                me
                this
            in
            "Cousin Bette"
    or was it
            Kerouac
                in
            "On the Road"
                    ?

411

gagaku

crack
   heads
walk (scurry
       shirtless)
back
  &
  forth

  over &
     over—
their
  skin
  sizzling

  in
chilly
     weather

gagaku

makes little difference—
Mozart composing
to his death—just
     to
have something
      to
       do

gagaku

I'll bet 78%
        of
written history
        is
    utter horse-
            shit

made up by cash
hungry
            academics

for good reason—
            to pay
for vittles.

gagaku

all th'false
    teeth
  on television

  all th'cosmetics

all th'sexy
  phony
        demons

on a show
  called
        "CHARMED"

my demons turn
        TV
            off
    then
      turn their face
            180°

  and eye me

  nothing phony about'em

gagaku

Aphrodite
        loves
      crack.

"crack for crack"
she told me.

        at
    least she loves
    something

gagaku

be a poet
50 years
    ahead
of yr time

    see
what's coming
      in
  all its
    frowzy
glory

     ahead
   of th'lame
    others

gagaku

th'first time
      I heard
 'inner gut'
it was Bukowski
    talking

 demons
   (mine?) close
their eyes——doze
right in front
      of me

 now
   quiver their eye
        lids

gagaku

could be demons
            are
        angels
masquerading
                to
            keep
        me
    occupied

gagaku

better to see demons
   and
write of 'em

that way they VENT

NO & YES they face
   gesture

Aphrodite knocked last night
         loud
   she wanted 10 dollars
         I
      didn't have it

     then 3 times again she
       knocked
           LOUD

     I didn't open
       for
     she was drunk
         demanding
       &
     obnoxious

   she is a SYLPH
      BUT
    sometimes
         SHRILL

gagaku

if you are
        TOO
        OPEN
        with her
                (Aphrodite)

    you
        will END
                UP
            in th'madhouse
                    or

            on
        skidrow

    it's not her fault

            it's
        just th'way she's

            channeled

gagaku

friday th'13th
my kind of day
      I live in a one
          room flop
  room #13
     they call it fourteen
         but
        it's 13

    my fucking demons?
         happy
      as apparent
           hell

     doing jumping jacks
skipping
        tattered rope
           too
   plus
    push-ups
          chin ups
    and?
      running in circles
          on
        no ground—

   NO
   GROUND
        at
       all

gagaku

god bless th'demons
th'devil take
      th'angels

   th'best poem?
      "ETERNITY"
          by
   Billy
      Blake

   &
   "FREEDOM"
by
   Charley
      Bukowski

my opinions couldn't be
      less widely
     deceminated (?)
   incinerated—

   my demons clap for me
    they're
        orderly
   mature
      mother-
        fuckers

gagaku

no goddamn sun
      this morn

   yes
      th'sun
         too
can be an
       ass
   hole

gagaku

demons
wave at me

still my only
                    friends

they keep me company